Teaching English in Italy

TEACHING ENGLISH
ITALY

Martin Penner

PASSPORT BOOKS
a division of *NTC Publishing Group*
Lincolnwood, Illinois USA

Published by Passport Books
a division of NTC Publishing Group
4255 West Touhy Avenue
Lincolnwood (Chicago), Illinois
60646-1975

ISBN 0-8442-0878-7
Library of Congress Catalog Card Number: on file

First published by In Print Publishing Ltd.
9 Beaufort Terrace
Brighton BN2 2SU
UK

Typeset by MC Typeset
Printed in the U.K. by Bell & Bain

To Elena

About the author

Martin Penner has taught English in Germany, Italy, and briefly in the Sudan. He started working in Italy in 1989 and since then he has taught in Potenza, Naples and Rome. He has worked privately, in an engineering company, for a private school, and on European Union educational development projects. At present, he teaches at International House/Accademia Britannica in Rome. As well as teaching, he writes articles for magazines and works as a freelance translator.

International House

International House (IH) began in 1953, when John and Brita Haycraft opened a language school in Cordoba, Spain. It has since developed into the largest independent British-based organization for teaching English, with over 100 000 students, 2 000 teachers, and some 90 schools around the world.

The home of the organization is International House in London, a non-profit-making eduational charity whose aim is to raise the standard of English teaching worldwide. Trustees include prominent academics, as well as representatives of the British Council, ARELS/FELCO and BBC English by Radio and Television.

International House in London, based at 106 Piccadilly, operates one of the principal schools of English in the UK, as well as International House Teacher Training. The latter offers a variety of courses leading to the UCLES/RSA Certificate and the UCLES/RSA Diploma, and courses for foreign teachers of English. It also offers specialized training courses – Teaching Business English, Development Course in Teacher Training, Director of Studies Training Course, etc. As well as being responsible for over half of the UCLES/RSA Certificate training in the world, International House Teacher Training is the sole body authorized to offer a Distance Training Programme leading to the UCLES/RSA Diploma in TEFLA.

International House in London is also the home of the Central Department, headquarters of the IH World Organization. This is an association of independent language schools and teacher training institutes which are affiliated to, but not owned by, the International House Trust. The Central Department supplies the affiliated schools with materials and advice on a wide range of educational and administrative matters, organizes annual conferences, and monitors standards. Through its Teacher Selection Department, IH recruits teachers and senior staff for the affiliated schools and other approved institutes.

The opinions expressed in this book are not necessarily those of IH, and, while every care has been taken to ensure accuracy, IH cannot accept responsibility for any errors or omissions.

Table of contents

PART 1
TEACHING JOBS AND HOW TO FIND THEM

PART 2
LIVING IN ITALY

Introduction

Presumably if you are reading this introduction, you are either in Italy already or are thinking about going there, so I will not waste time listing its attractions or the reasons you might have for going. Suffice it to say, Italy has been for many years one of the most popular destinations for teachers of English, and few regret the decision to go and work there.

This book is designed to give you the practical help you need to make a move to Italy as trouble-free as possible. **Part 1** deals with the business of finding jobs and gives you a picture of what the opportunities are. **Part 2** covers what you need to know not only before you go, but also in the first months when you are trying to find your feet in a culture which, for all its similarities with the English-speaking world, still has its enigmatic qualities. **Part 3** is about the nitty-gritty of teaching English to Italians. If you are already a teacher with some experience, parts of it will be well known to you. Even if this is the case, the sections dealing with Italian students in particular should help you get to grips with the specific problems and characteristics of the students you will find in front of you.

There are also seven **Appendices** at the back of the book which may be useful for reference. They include case studies of five English teachers and interviews with two more.

It is unlikely that you will make a fortune teaching English in Italy. On the other hand it is very likely that you will have a lot of fun, and gain much professionally. You will also see the country from the inside and arrive at an understanding of its people which goes beyond the usual stereotypical images of excitable, spaghetti-slurping *Mafiosi*.

Martin Penner

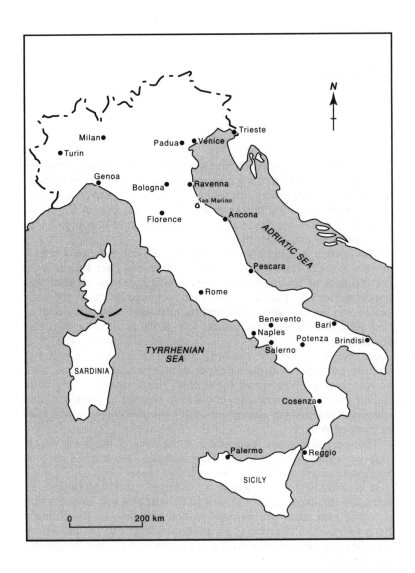

Part 1

TEACHING JOBS AND HOW TO FIND THEM

1 | Courses and qualifications

Once upon a time in Italy getting jobs teaching English was the easiest thing in the world. No experience or qualifications were required – it was enough to be a native speaker. Times have changed and it is no longer so easy to walk into teaching jobs. This is partly because the boom in the EFL (English as a Foreign Language) industry has reached a plateau, partly because there are now hundreds of prospective teachers already in Italy, and also because Italian school-owners have, for the most part, wised-up. Many schools require you to have either two years' experience, or the RSA certificate in TEFLA (see below) before they will consider taking you on. This does not mean that you will not get any work without them. It does, however, mean that you will probably be barred access to the established, reputable schools and the better-paid company jobs.

RSA/UCLES Preparatory Certificate in TEFLA

(RSA is the Royal Society of Arts; UCLES is the University of Cambridge Local Examinations Syndicate; and TEFLA is Teaching English as a Foreign Language to Adults.) This is the qualification which is recognized throughout the world as proof of basic competence in teaching English. In Italy all employers will know what it is, and you will have much more success in your job-hunt with it than without it.

The courses usually last four weeks (full-time) and they give you a good grounding in the basic techniques and methods of English teaching. Although there is no guarantee of a job afterwards, at the end of the course some help and guidelines are offered for finding jobs. Most people find work within a month of finishing the course.

Courses cost around £750 and are often advertised in the UK in the *Guardian* and the *Independent* newspapers. It is possible to do courses all around the world, including the USA and Australia, but the UK (and London especially) offers by far the most training centres. For information contact:

3

> *UK*: International House, London (tel: 071 491 2598). *For details of IH centres around the world, contact Central Department, 071 499 5848.*
> *USA*: English International, Inc, San Francisco (tel: 415 749 5633).
> *Australia*: Australian College of English, Sydney (tel: 02 389 0133).

In addition to the UK, courses are run in IH centres in Australia, Austria, Czech Republic, Egypt, France, Hungary, Italy, Poland, Portugal, Spain, and the USA. For information on other courses contact UCLES in the UK (tel: 0223 61111) who can provide a full list of centres worldwide.

If you want to do a course in Italy, some of the major centres are:

> *Rome*: Accademia Britannica (International House), Viale Manzoni 57 (tel: 06 70476894).
> *Milan*: British School, Via Montenapoleone 5 (tel: 02 780741).
> *Trieste*: British School of Trieste, Via Torrebianca 18 (tel: 040 369369).

Beware of ads for TEFL training courses which do not mention RSA or UCLES, or some other officially recognized body. It may be that they offer sound training (though this is not guaranteed), but they may not be officially recognized abroad. If you have a Post Graduate Certificate in Education (PGCE) or equivalent qualification, you may not need anything else to find a satisfactory job – similarly a Bachelor of Education (B Ed) degree will be taken into account by English-speaking teacher selectors.

When you have been teaching for a few years you may want to consider doing the RSA/UCLES Diploma in TEFLA. This takes you further into the theory and practice of teaching and is a virtual guarantee of work. You will need this if you intend to climb the TEFL career ladder.

2 Job possibilities

Teaching privately

Teaching privately may well be (or seem) more profitable than working for an organization. There are some disadvantages however: you have to find the work yourself; you have to sort out premises, materials, times, and prices on your own; theoretically you are supposed to complete tax forms and make insurance payments yourself (in reality this rarely happens); you have little security as people often cancel at the last minute, for which you lose money and waste time; travelling can be a bind if clients expect you to go to them.

You should remember that you are likely to have private work for only seven or eight months of the year, as during the summer in Italy everyone goes away and nobody can be bothered to learn English.

You should also consider the implications of teaching privately for your CV, as in the future, prospective employers are less likely to be impressed by previous employment which often cannot be 'proved', or provide you with an official reference. The same problem arises if you want to do the RSA/UCLES Diploma, for which you would need 2 years' proven experience, preferably in a language school.

On the other hand, teaching privately means you are in control of everything, so you can take holidays when you like, organize your working day to suit you and, to a certain extent, teach what you like to whom you like.

If you manage to get a group of private students together, then teaching can be really lucrative. A group of six, each paying 10 000 lire (very cheap) is 60 000 lire per hour – more than you are ever likely to get from an individual, and much more than you will get from a school. The problem here is that friends often want to study together even if they are at completely different levels, and many groups disintegrate rapidly once the initial enthusiasm has worn off.

Most teachers in Italy have one main job with a school and top up their salaries with a few privates. It is difficult to live off private lessons alone.

Private language schools

This is where the majority of English teachers work most of the time. Within the sphere of private language schools there is a wide range of teaching available: some teach only adults, but the tendency nowadays is to run courses for children and teenagers too, and most schools do a proportion of their work in companies as well as in the school itself.

The advantages of working for a school are obvious. You have a structure to work within, with all the support which that provides, and it is also more secure than working privately. Most schools guarantee you a certain number of hours per week so that you have a minimum income fixed.

Also, within a school environment you have the possibility of making headway in a career in TEFL, if that is what you want. All schools have some sort of teacher hierarchy. In established schools, there is often a recognized scale, starting with new teachers and moving up through senior teachers to the position of Director of Studies. In other schools it will be less well defined, but in either case teachers who stay with one school or organization, are likely with time to move up through the ranks, and naturally salaries increase accordingly. Furthermore a good school, with a Director of Studies, can provide you with the educational support that you will need to develop as a teacher.

To turn to practical matters, most of the teaching in private schools tends to be in the late afternoon and evening, sometimes until 10 pm. This is because people generally attend English courses after work. During the day classes are few and far between, limited to housewives and students who are the only people free at these times. If your school sends you out to work in a company, then you may be working in the early afternoon, but even here morning work is very unusual.

On average students have two 90–120 minute lessons per week, although in the summer intensive courses (several hours every day) are also common. Classes can contain as few as 4 or 5 students, and the maximum is usually 15. Teachers generally work between 20 and 30 hours per week if they are full-time; part-time can mean anything from 2 or 3 hours to 15 or 20. Although some teachers work for more than one school, this can be inconvenient as timetables tend to clash and a lot of time is spent travelling.

The precise details of contracts and working conditions vary enormously and these are discussed at length in subsequent chapters.

Companies

With a lot of initiative and some luck it is possible to get yourself taken on by a company as an in-house language instructor. There are no fixed channels for finding this type of work, apart from going through the phone-book, finding the big companies and presenting yourself. It is difficult work to get as firms often want the security of someone with an established company or organization behind them. Besides there are relatively few firms with the resources to employ an English teacher full-time. If they want teachers, it is usually by the hour and they approach schools for this. Occasionally they will hire people privately for a few hours' tuition every week, and in these cases it is a question of knowing the right people and being in the right place at the right time.

Teachers in companies tend to find that students are not adequately divided into levels and motivation can be a problem if people are forced to come against their will. Despite this rather negative picture, plenty of people do work in companies and it can be rewarding, financially and professionally.

Universities

All Italian universities employ native speakers as *lettori*. It is not just the language faculties which require them; English has become part of almost all degree programmes because of its dominant role in books, reference works and international conferences. So within one university there may be three or four possibilities.

In general *lettori* work about 10 hours per week on full-time contracts. Holidays are long and the pay is good. Naturally there is a lot of competition for these posts.

On the downside, classes can be huge – a hundred or more is very common. They are also completely diverse in terms of level, with the average student at about intermediate level. Obviously, with such little contact and in such conditions, it is hard to develop much of a relationship with individual students. People who work in universities say that it is a very different kind of teaching to that done in schools and it takes some getting used to.

To apply to a university, find out which faculties take English *lettori* and write to the *Preside* (Dean of the faculty), stating who you are and which academic year you are interested in. Include a CV/resumé and copies of all your educational qualifications. April and May are the best months to apply, when the authorities start thinking about the new academic year.

3 Finding a job

If you want to teach English in Italy, there are two things you can do: (1) try to get a job before you go or (2) simply go, and then look for a job.

The first option can be difficult, but it has obvious advantages in that it makes the business of getting started in Italy that much easier. For example, your flight will probably be paid for you and you will no doubt get some help in finding accommodation. It can be difficult, however, because many schools prefer to recruit teachers on the spot, where they can see you and you can see them. Only a small percentage of job openings are advertised abroad. To be taken on from abroad you will almost definitely need a teaching qualification. Employers understandably want some sort of guarantee that you will be able to do the job.

The second option – going to Italy and then looking for work – is more nerve-racking, and more expensive than the first. Nevertheless it is the way many teachers go about it, and it has several advantages. You have immediate access to many more job possibilities than you would at home. You are in a position to check them out thoroughly and in person. If you are short on qualifications or experience, you have more chance of finding work. And finally, by doing everything yourself you are less likely to find yourself in a job or apartment you don't like.

FINDING WORK BEFORE YOU GO

To get a decent job from outside Italy, you need a qualification. An RSA certificate in TEFLA is the most widely recognized, but B Eds and PGCEs may also satisfy. That said, you can then try the following strategies to find work.

Methods

Contact International House Teacher Selection Department in the UK (tel: 071-491-2598). IH has affiliated schools throughout Italy. Minimum requirements are RSA/UCLES CTEFLA Pass A or B, or an equivalent qualification. Teachers with a Pass C also need a year's experience. Apart from recruiting teachers, it can also offer careers advice.

Use your training institute. If you do a course in an established TEFL training centre, apart from giving you advice on where to look for work, they may also have a jobs noticeboard with vacancies advertised for countries all over the world. Also ask tutors if they have any contacts in Italy. There is bound to be someone who has worked in Italy and who can give you useful advice, if not names and addresses.

Send your CV and a letter of enquiry to any schools you can locate. Start with the schools listed in Appendix 3, prioritizing the ones which are part of large organizations. These are more likely to recruit people from outside Italy.

Check newspapers for job ads. In the UK, the *Guardian* (Tuesdays), the *Times Educational Supplement* (Fridays) and the *Independent* all have a regular TEFL job section. The *EFL Gazette* carries job ads, but you have to have it sent to you (contact 0202 699462 for details). In the USA the *TESOL Placement Bulletin* has lists of teaching jobs which they will send to you for a fee (contact TESOL Inc, 1600 Cameron Street, Suite 300, Alexandria, VA 22314; tel: 703 836 0774).

Try an agency. To be registered with an agency you normally need at least the RSA certificate. If you send the agency your CV it will put you in a databank, and give you a call when a suitable vacancy comes up. Although all but one of the following are in the UK, they can still be used by non-British job-hunters. Telephone first just to check procedure as it can vary slightly:

> **The Connor TEFL Register**, Via Settembrini 1, 20124 Milan, Italy (tel: 02 6700774).
>
> **Bell Educational Trust**, Overseas Dept, The Lodge, Redcross Lane, Cambridge CB2 2QX, UK (tel: 0223 246644).
>
> **Anchor Language Services**, 30 Brick Row, Babraham, Cambridge CB2 4AJ, UK (tel: 0223 836017).
>
> **ELT Banbury**, 49 Oxford Road, Banbury, Oxon OX16 9AH, UK (tel: 0295 263480).
>
> **English Worldwide**, 17 New Concordia Wharf, Mill St, London SE1 2BB, UK (tel: 071 252 1402).
>
> **Language School Appointments**, 27 Delancey Street, London NW1 7RX, UK (tel: 071 388 6644).
>
> **Nord-Anglia International Ltd**, 10 Eden Place, Cheadle, Stockport, Cheshire SK8 1AT, UK (tel: 061 491 4191).

Contact the recruitment agencies operated by Berlitz, Inlingua and Linguarama. These are large language school chains which sometimes recruit teachers in the UK or USA, and usually give recruits a training course in their own method of teaching. (NB: These methods do not suit everyone and may be rather different from approaches introduced on a UCLES 4-week course.) Contact addresses are:

> **Berlitz (UK)**, Wells House, 79 Wells Street, London W1P 3RE, UK (tel: 071 580 6482). Also, 101 The Piazza, Piccadilly Plaza, Manchester M1 4BW, UK (tel: 061 228 3607).
> **Berlitz (US)**, Research Park, 239 Wall Street, Princeton, NJ 08540. USA.
> **Inlingua**, Rodney Lodge, Rodney Road, Cheltenham GL50 1JF, UK (tel: 0242 253171).
> **Linguarama**, Oceanic House, 89 High Street, Alton, Hants GU34 1LG, UK (tel: 0962 854488).

Best time to look

April, May and June are the best months to look for jobs as this is when existing teachers decide they are going to move on for the new academic year (September–July), and so employers start looking for replacements.

Interviews

If you are asked for an interview, prepare to emphasize your interest in languages, your love of working with people and your lively, cheerful nature. Also be prepared to answer a few questions on teaching methodology. Interviewers do not always ask questions on this, but if they do it is good to have a couple of model lesson plans up your sleeve.

Finally, use the opportunity to find out as much as possible about the school or the job concerned. It is unwise to accept any job until you know exactly how much money you are going to get, in your hand, every month.

FINDING WORK WHEN YOU ARRIVE

Most people who come to Italy looking for teaching work find something relatively quickly. What they find initially may not be ideal, but it starts some money coming in, and creates a base from which to move towards a better situation.

Best time to look

September and October are the months when you have the best chance of finding good jobs. This is when courses start up, and schools find they do not have sufficient teachers. There is another wave of activity in January when new courses start and some teachers do not return after Christmas.

Blocking time

It is not always possible to find one job straight away which pays enough to live on. You may find a few hours' work in several different places, meaning that you have to do a lot of travelling, and put up with some very long days, to earn a reasonable wage.

As time goes on, and as you impress people with your professionalism, you will probably be offered more hours by some of your employers. Then begins a difficult stage of accepting some and refusing others as you try to get yourself a pleasant weekly timetable which involves the minimum of travelling, which pays reasonably well and offers some job satisfaction. Obviously the key here is to keep your nose scrupulously clean with those people you want to give you more work.

It may be six months or so before you manage to 'block' all your work in such a way that you start at a certain time, work solidly for five or six hours and then stop for the day. However, with perseverance and a little good judgment you should get there in the end. Be careful about accepting work in the late afternoon and early evening. This is when most people will be willing to give you work, and so you will not want to waste those 'prime time' hours on a job that is awkward or pays badly.

Methods

Go to the English language bookshop in your city (addresses are given in the section below on 'What to look for when job-hunting – accommodation'). There you can pick up whatever English-language newspapers are produced locally and consult them for job ads. In Rome ask for *Wanted in Rome* or the *Metropolitan*, while in Milan there is *The Informer*.

There are often also noticeboards in the English bookshops. Knowing that prospective teachers are bound to pass by, schools often advertise jobs here.

Go through the Yellow Pages (look under *Scuole di Lingue*) and contact all the schools you can find. It is probably best to ring first, talk to the Director of Studies and try to fix an appointment to go round, present your CV and have a chat. If you meet people in person, you have more chance of being remembered when a job comes up.

Through contacts. Contacts can do more than the most stunning CV, so the more you make the better. Make a point of going to expat haunts and try to get talking to other teachers. Most will have been in your situation at some point, so they will probably be ready to give you any advice they can. The Irish pub is a good place to start, because there is one in every city and they are always well attended. In Rome try the **Fiddler's Elbow**, Via del Omarta 43; or **The Fox**, Via Monterone 19. In Milan, look in at **Bar Magenta**, Largo D'Ancona; **Bar Matricola**, Viale Romagna 43; or **Racanà**, Via Sannio.

Private lessons. This is a good way to make some money if things are going badly. Go to the university, the English bookshops, and your local bar and *alimentari* and put up notices offering English lessons. Something like this should do the trick:

> Insegnante Madrelingua
> Impartisce lezioni di
> INGLESE a gruppi o individui.
> Prezzi moderati
> Telefonare al 123 456

Find out from other teachers in the city what the going rate is, so that you do not either price yourself out of the market or undersell your services. You could also try putting an ad in the local newspaper, although it might prove expensive.

In the normal course of things, foreigners tend to get asked for private lessons anyway, by friends, acquaintances and strangers on the bus. The trick is to tell who are likely to stay the course and who will fade away after two or three lessons.

Professional Women's Association (Milan only). This is an organization which helps English-speaking women find jobs. Contact Tracey Morton on 02 38001127.

WHAT TO LOOK FOR WHEN JOB-HUNTING

This section is concerned primarily with private language schools, where the bulk of the job opportunities available to foreign English teachers are to be found. What follows is a list of things you should find out about a school and the job it is offering before you accept any employment. If you are aware of all these things, you should avoid nasty surprises.

How many hours? For a full-time position you should have a maximum of 25 contact hours a week. Any more will be bad for you and your teaching. 'Contact hours' refers to time actually in the classroom with students. Taking preparation into account, a 25-hour teaching load represents a 40-hour week at least.

How are they dispersed? Make sure that the hours to be worked are blocked reasonably well – that is, not spaced out over morning, afternoon and evening. Most good schools will do what they can to facilitate this, but you may need to be flexible if you really want a particular job.

Class type and size. First, will you be expected to teach adults or children (if so, what ages) or both? Second, is it mostly general English, or business English or ESP (English for Specific Purposes)? Third, what are the different levels of English according to which classes are organized? And how are students assigned to a particular level? Fourth, what are the minimum and maximum numbers in a class? A good school will have a proper placement system and relatively low class maximum (15 or 16).

In school or in companies? Find out if the job involves teaching in the school, in companies, or some of each. If there is company teaching, what are the companies? Where are they? Are the lessons one-to-one with managers or with groups? What sort of facilities are available there (video, tape-recorder, photocopier)?

Travelling time. An important thing to consider is how much time you would spend travelling to the school if you accepted the job. Also, if they send you outside to teach, how much travelling will it involve? And is travelling time paid? Or the cost of the trip?

Rate of pay. Average rates of pay in schools are: 20 000–25 000 lire per hour or 1.5 million lire per month. As well as averages, these are minimum figures for a reasonable existence in a city. In smaller towns you can get by on less because rents are less. First, find out if you will be paid by the hour or a fixed salary every month. If the first is the case, how many hours are you guaranteed, if any? And what happens if a class is cancelled for some reason? Whether the offer is a salary or an hourly rate, make sure you are being told the net pay, after taxes have been deducted.

Holidays. How much time off do you get for Christmas, Easter and summer? Remember that unless you are being offered a full-time contract it is very unlikely that you will be paid for the time when you are not working. So, pleasant as it may seem to have long holidays, what it probably means is long periods with no income.

Contract? Schools which give their teachers proper contracts are in the minority in Italy, because contracts involve expense and inconvenience for the employer. The main advantage of a contract is the security of having a fixed salary twelve or thirteen times per year. Details of how contracts work are given in a later section in this chapter.

Accommodation. Most schools do not offer their teachers accommodation, free or otherwise. Schools that recruit locally assume that prospective teachers already have somewhere fixed to live. Nevertheless it is worth asking about accommodation because other teachers might know of something, or they might let you leave an advert on the noticeboard. If a school is recruiting you from abroad, however, it should find you somewhere to stay, at least to start with. If it does not, it shows very little commitment from the employer and does not bode well for the future of your working relationship.

Library, materials. Ask about what sort of back-up teachers have in terms of facilities and materials. Is there a library of books for teachers to consult? This is one of the things that will indicate how much concern there is for the teachers' welfare and professional development.

Teacher's room. This can be another indication of how much importance is accorded to the teaching staff in the school. If there is not one, it is probably the sort of school where you come in, do your teaching and then go again, without much contact with anyone. If you are already settled in the particular town, with an independent social life, this may be fine. If you are new, to teaching and to Italy, you probably want advice on all sorts of things and also a space to relax and make friends in. The presence of a room for teachers means that there is some bond felt between teachers, and as a result the school is a much pleasanter place to work.

Self study centre. This is a place where students can go to study outside lesson times. It is usually equipped with tape-recorders with headphones, exercises of all types, newspapers, dictionaries, etc. As it is quite an undertaking to set up and run a self study centre, if there is one it is a sign that the school is serious about helping students progress.

AISLI (Associazione Italiana di Scuole di Lingue). This is an association of language schools in Italy which permits membership only to schools which satisfy its standards of teaching and organization. Inspectors come round regularly to check standards and as a result AISLI (pronounced 'eyes-lee') schools can be relied on to be worth working for. Note that this does not mean that any school which is not a member is automatically rubbish. Many schools which are part of very reputable organizations like International House and the British Schools Group are not members. However, it does provide a useful guide to small unaffiliated schools, many of which are very sound but some of which are not. If a school is not a member, you can judge a lot about it from what is said about AISLI. So ask anyway. If they have never heard of it, you are not talking to one of the best.

CONTRACT OR FREELANCE?

As mentioned above, the vast majority of English teachers in Italy do not have contracts. This is because only universities and a few very well established schools offer them. While there are definite advantages to having one, it is by no means necessary and you can have a perfectly satisfactory job without one. If you find you are in a position to choose whether to have one or not, it is as well to know exactly what is involved. The following summary should help you to know where you stand, whether you end up working on contract or freelance.

Contracts

The obvious advantage in having a contract is job security. If you have a contract, you are classed as a *dipendente* of your company and as a result you have certain privileges. For example, you cannot be fired without notice.

Most schools which give their teachers contracts adhere to the national teachers' contract. Others work out their own which may or may not be similar. The first thing you should find out if you are being offered a contract is whether or not it is the national one. If not, look very carefully at the conditions. A standard national contract stipulates a certain number of hours to be worked per week and guarantees a fixed salary in thirteen payments per year (that is, twelve monthly salary payments and the so-called *tre-*

dicessima which is the equivalent of a salary payment and is usually given just before Christmas.

On top of this, the school or institute undertakes to pay all the necessary taxes (health and insurance contributions) for you. If you are a citizen of the European Union this means that what you pay in Italy is valid for the national benefit schemes in your own country too. Often contracts work on what is called a *monte ore* system. This means that you have to work a certain number of hours in the year, but the number of hours per week can vary according to the time of year and the amount of work available. The maximum number of hours per week is stipulated (usually about 30).

On the downside, your holidays are limited both in terms of when you can take them and how many days you can have (usually about 35 a year).

Freelance

At first sight it may seem that you can earn more working freelance than you can with a contract. An average contract will give you about 1.5 million lire per month, while 25 hours per week freelance, at 20 000 lire net per hour, gives you at least 2 million.

If you work freelance, however, you have to remember that you are only going to get paid that sum for 9 or 10 months of the year. You do not get paid during the summer, or at Christmas or Easter, when there is very little work about. Also, if you are ill, you will not be paid for the time you miss.

As far as taxes are concerned, the situation is more complicated than if you are on contract. Nineteen per cent of your hourly rate is taken off at source by your employer. This money, called the *ritenuta d'acconto*, is paid to the government as income tax, but it does not entitle you to health care, for which you have to make your own arrangements (see section on 'Health'). Theoretically you should make an income declaration (*dichiarazione dei redditi*) at the end of the fiscal year, and then pay extra tax if you have earned into a higher wage bracket. As the limits of the brackets frequently change, you will need expert advice. In practice, however, there is little control on this, and foreigners especially tend to get by without doing it.

The advantages of working freelance are the freedom it gives you to switch employers and take long holidays if you want. If you are intending to stay for only a short time, you can earn money without too much bureaucratic wrangling, and without any official documents except your *Codice Fiscale*. Documents are dealt with in the next chapter.

4 | Documents

Getting a job as an English teacher in Italy is fairly straightforward. Getting all the documents and papers which say you are doing it legally is not. The list of documents and certificates which you could and should in theory have is a good deal longer than your arm.

In practice teachers tend to limit themselves to what they need. If you are a footloose globe-trotter you can probably get by for months, even years with nothing but your passport. At the other extreme if you are planning on spending some time in Italy you will have to get at least five or six documents done because as soon as you want to do anything, like get a decent job, pay tax, get a doctor, you start needing handfuls of them.

Below you will find the most important documents for day-to-day living in Italy. They are (more or less) in the order in which you will need them. I have also included basic details about where and how to get them. If you have any problems finding the various offices in your town, take a look at *Tutto Città*. This is a book of maps and important information issued by the phone company to every household in every town in Italy. At the front you will find a section entitled *Documenti: dove farli* which will list all the documents you could possibly need along with the addresses and phone numbers of the relevant offices in your locality.

One final word. Italian bureaucracy is Kafka-esque at the best of times. Double-check that on every document you are issued your name and particulars are exactly correct. Any slight discrepancies can cause bureaucratic nightmares.

Permesso di Soggiorno

This is your stay permit and according to the law anyone who wants to spend any time in Italy has to have one, even tourists. In the case of English teachers, it is possible to get by without one for a few months, but as soon as you start earning money you are breaking nearly every rule in the book. It is also worth bearing in mind the fact that you have virtually no rights without one.

If you are employed by a school, company or anyone else, your employer should give you a letter stating the fact. The authorities will want to see this before issuing your *Permesso*. If you are working freelance it is much more difficult because you are entitled only to a 'tourist' permit and theoretically this does not allow you to work. In practice, however, this is how many foreigners resolve the problem.

Where to go? The *Permesso* is obtained from **Questura, Ufficio Stranieri** (the foreign office of the local police station). This is generally open mornings only, from Monday to Saturday. Among the largest are:

> *Rome* – Via Genova
> *Milan* – Via Fatebenefratelli 11
> *Naples* – Via Medina 75

What to take? You will need:

- Your passport and a photocopy of it.
- A letter from your employer (saying that they are employing you).
- 2 passport photos.
- A special tax stamp (*marca da bollo*) for Lit 10 000 which you can obtain at most tobacconists.

Other points. Try to get to the *Questura* as early as possible. The recent influx of Third World immigrants into Italy has sent the demand for *Permessi di Soggiorno* through the roof, resulting in huge queues and much frustration.

You will not get the permit straight away. Officials will tell you to come back in two or three weeks when your request has been processed. Best leave it a month, especially if you are in a big city.

Do not be surprised if at some point you feel like bursting into tears. This is perfectly normal. Just don't think it will earn you any favours.

Residenza

If you intend staying more than six months it is very advisable to obtain Residency. This is simply official recognition that you live where you do and means that your name and address are on a computer somewhere.

Apart from the stress of actually getting your name on the computer there are few disadvantages and several advantages. With Residency you are:

- Entitled to health assistance through the USSL (Unità Socio-Sanitaria Locale).
- Entitled to an Italian Identity Card. This is more useful than you would imagine. You tend to get stopped all over the place in Italy and the first thing the police want to see is some ID. A *Carta d'Identità* is smaller than a passport and so more convenient to carry round and the police like it because it is obviously Italian.
- Enabled to do things like buy houses, cars, land, convert your driving licence (without Residency you are not entitled to do any of these).

One problem with getting Residency is that many landlords only let apartments and houses to *non-residenti*. They do this for all sorts of legal reasons which are too boring to go into. To get round it there are two possibilities: don't tell your landlord or register yourself as resident at a friend's house. Both of these happen all the time, and neither are considered illegal.

Where to go? You need to go to your city's **Ufficio dell'Anagrafe** which is usually part of the town hall (*Comune*). In most cities there are several offices, one for each district. Once inside, look for signs which say things like *Stranieri*, *Domande di Residenza* or *Cambio Residenza*.

What to take? You will need:

- Your passport, plus a photocopy.
- Your *Permesso di Soggiorno*, plus a photocopy.
- Some cities will not issue you *Residenza* unless you prove payment of the local Rubbish Tax (*rifiuti solidi urbani*). If your landlord has not paid it and he will not be persuaded to do so, either you pay it yourself or forego *Residenza* in that particular place.

Other Points. After handing over all your information you will have to wait two or three months before you are officially resident.

No one will tell you if there are any problems with your application (like its having been lost). Even if you do not need the certificate, you would be wise to go back after a few months and check that your name is on the computer.

Every time you need to prove your residency you will have to go to the office, pay for a certificate and get it printed out on the computer. You cannot just keep the same one because they are valid for only three months, and anyway whoever wants to see it usually takes it from you.

Codice Fiscale

This is your tax code and you will need one before any reputable school or company will give you money as payment for services. As with the rest of these documents it is possible to get by without it, but if you do this you limit your job possibilities severely and it will be hard to be taken seriously without one. Given that this is one of the simplest things to do, it is well worth the effort.

Where to go? You obtain the *Codice Fiscale* from the **Ufficio Distrettuale delle Imposte Dirette**. In most places this is open from 8.30 until midday. If you do not know where it is, it will be in the phone book.

What to take? All you need is your passport plus a photocopy of it.

Other points. In most places this will be issued immediately or after a short wait (an hour at most).

You will be given a piece of card with the number on, and also a piece of plastic like a credit card, showing the same number.

Double-check that you have filled in all your personal details correctly. It is a criminal offence to give false information.

Libretto di Lavoro

The *Libretto di Lavoro* is a Labour Card stating that you are available and fit for work in Italy. Theoretically you should have it before you start working, but in practice this very rarely happens.

Many teachers do not bother getting a Labour Card because it is fairly easy and safe to get by without it. You really need it only if you are going to be taken on as a *dipendente* by your employer. Many schools and companies refuse to do this because it involves a lot of bureaucratic wrangling and more taxes. It is much easier to employ teachers as *liberi professionisti* (freelance) and leave all the fiscal and bureaucratic hassle to them. For what to do in this case, see the section below, on *Partita IVA*.

Where to go? You need to go to the *Comune* in your town, **Ufficio Libretto di Lavoro**, open mornings Monday to Friday.

What to take? You will need the following:
- Certificate of Residence.
- Some ID (passport is the safest).
- Degree certificate, or certificates for the last educational qualification you received. In some places this is no longer neces-

sary, which probably means that the rules are changing – but it is better not to take anything for granted so take them along with you.

Other points. Believe it or not, the *Libretto di Lavoro* is generally issued immediately, and the document is valid for all your working life.

For people outside the European Union it is incredibly hard to get and the vast majority of Americans, Canadians, Australians, and New Zealanders simply do not bother. If you are not a European Union citizen and you really want your Labour Card, ask at your embassy about the correct procedure and prepare for a lot of hassle (also see next section, on *Nulla Osta*).

Nulla Osta

Nulla Osta, which means 'no obstacle', is a permit granted by the Italian state authorizing an employer to take on a person as a *dipendente*. Despite the fact that it is your company or school which needs it, you are the one that has to do all the leg work involved in getting it issued.

The *Nulla Osta*, most inconveniently, has to be obtained after you have found a job, and theoretically before you start work. Generally schools let you work immediately, on the understanding that you get the *Nulla Osta* as soon as possible.

Where to go? The *Nulla Osta* is obtained from the **Ufficio di Collocamento** (Employment Office) for your town. They are usually open from 9.00 until 12.30, and they are always crowded, so get there as early as you can.

What to take? You will need:

- *Permesso di Soggiorno.*
- *Libretto di Lavoro.*
- *Codice Fiscale.*
- An ID document.
- An Employment Request, *Richiesta di Assunzione*, completed by your employer (your school or company should prepare this for you as it is rather complicated).

Other points. The *Nulla Osta* is issued immediately and lasts as long as you are employed by the employer stated on it.

If you manage to crack this one, congratulations! You've gone as far as you can go. You now have all the rights of an Italian citizen and may consider yourself completely legal (and hence in a minority).

Partita IVA

This is what you will need if you are not taken on as a *dipendente* by your employer, and are thus classed as freelance. Without it you will not be *in regole* (doing it by the book). 'Not doing it by the book' is an Italian speciality and when you see the complicated (and expensive) procedure which the law demands, you will see why.

Basically the *Partita IVA* consists of a number, rather like a VAT number, which you have to put on an invoice every time someone pays you for your services. You are also required to get special invoice and expenses registers from official stationers and to make a tax declaration every year on a form called the '740'. Needless to say thousands of Italians do not do any of this and many English teachers find that, at least in the short term, they are better off without it. You will have to discuss it with your conscience and see if you can face the ordeal. If you do decide to go by the book, I strongly recommend that you find an Italian to help you fill in the various forms and to explain exactly what you have to do.

Where to go? You need to go to the **Ufficio Provinciale IVA** (see the phone book or *Tuttocittà*). They are generally open mornings only from Monday to Saturday.

What to take? You will need:

- *Codice Fiscale*.
- Some ID, plus a photocopy.
- Proof of payment of Lit 100 000 to the Post Office account of the *Ufficio IVA*. You can pay this at any Post Office.

Other points. Your *Partita IVA* is valid until you decide to close it, but you still have to pay Lit 100 000 per year for 'running costs'.

If you get involved with *IVA* you will soon hear of ways people get round it. They may work, but they are all illegal.

Something often mentioned in this field is the *Ritenuta d'Acconto*. This is a system whereby 19% of the money you are paid is deducted and paid to the government on your behalf. What you are then supposed to do is make a tax declaration at the end of the year (the famous form 740) and the government will tell you if you have to pay any more or not. There are several problems with this. First, it is valid only up to a certain earnings limit (which is lower than what you will need to get by on). Second, it can be used only three or four times per year, otherwise it becomes obvious that you are working on a regular freelance basis and hence you should have a *Partita IVA*. Third, schools have been known to tell teachers they are taking off the 19% for *Ritenuta d'Acconto* and then not pay it. They then 'forget' to give the ignorant teacher the proof that the payments have been made, leaving him or her out of pocket and outside the law.

Non-EU citizens

Thanks to increasingly strict immigration laws, citizens outside the European Union have a terrible time getting legal in Italy. For the most part, they simply don't and work *nero* (illegally). The official process by which non-EU nationals come to work in Italy is a marathon of bureaucracy and makes the procedure for Europeans look like a tea-party. It goes something like this.

You arrive in Italy for reasons of Tourism (you are not allowed to come for anything else), and then by lucky chance you come across a company or school wishing to take you on. Alternatively, before you come you find an employer in Italy willing to employ you. Either way, the employer then has to petition the Labour Office on your behalf, asking if they can take you on instead of one of the thousands of Italians looking for work. The Labour Office issues the permit, which is presented to the police who 'investigate' for a while. Then, whether you are in Italy or at home, you must go in person to the Italian consulate in Australia, the USA, Canada or New Zealand and make a request to work in Italy. Unfortunately, despite the fact that this means a journey halfway round the world just for a piece of paper, the law allows no way around the regulation. When and if your request is accepted you can start at square one – applying for a *Permesso di Lavoro* (see above).

5 | Before you go

This chapter deals with basic travel information, useful preparatory steps, and what to take out to Italy with you.

PRACTICAL PREPARATION

Finding a flight

If you have been recruited in your home country, some employers will arrange, and pay for your flight. Otherwise, if you are flying from the UK, avoid major airlines like BA and Alitalia. You will almost certainly find cheaper flights which are just as convenient. For the best deals, look in the classified ad section of the *Sunday Times*, *Observer*, *Time Out* and the *Evening Standard*. There are also several agencies specializing in flights to Italy (see below) and other student/youth organizations (see below) which should be able to find you a return flight for about £130 in the low season and under £200 in the high.

Some UK travel agents offering cheapish flights to Italy are:

> **Campus Travel**, 52 Grosvenor Gardens, London SW1 0AG (tel: 071 730 3402). There are other offices in Bristol, Cambridge, Edinburgh and Oxford.
> **CTS Travel**, 44 Goodge St, London W1P 1FH (tel: 071 637 5601).
> **Italflights**, 125 High Holborn, London WC1V 6QA (tel: 071 405 6771).
> **Italia Nel Mondo**, 6 Palace St, London SW1E 5HY (tel: 071 834 7651).
> **Nouvelles Frontières**, 11 Blenheim St, London W1Y 0QP (tel: 071 629 7772).
> **STA Travel**, 86 Old Brompton Road, London SW7 3LQ; 117 Euston Road, London NW1 2SX (tel: 071 937 9921). There are also offices in Bristol, Cambridge, Oxford and Manchester.

From Ireland: at the time of writing there are no regular direct flights between Ireland and Italy. The best solution seems to be to get to London and go from there.

From Australia and New Zealand: direct flights with Quantas and Garuda (from Australia) and Garuda and Thai (from New Zealand) connect Melbourne, Sydney and Auckland with Rome. From Australia, flights are about Aus$2200 in the high season and Aus$1700 in the low; from New Zealand about NZ$2900 high to NZ$2300 low. STA Travel has offices in many major cities and will find you the cheapest option available. STA Head Offices in Australia and New Zealand are:

> *Australia*: 224 Faraday St, Carlton 3053, Melbourne (tel: 03 347 4711).
> *New Zealand*: 10 High St, Auckland (tel: 09 309 9723).

From North America: although many people fly to Italy via the UK there are plenty of direct flights available, generally to Milan or Rome. To save money, plan to travel low season (late October to early April), avoiding weekends if possible. If you buy a ticket direct from an airline (see below) you will have a wide range of travel dates and destinations available but you will pay more than you would with a discount flight agent. On the other hand the latter may not have a flight exactly as you would like it. Check the Sunday newspapers for cheap flights or contact your nearest STA Travel agent (see below). Airlines include:

> **Alitalia**, 666 Fifth Avenue, New York, NY 10103, USA (tel: 212 582 8900); 2055 Peel St, Montréal, Quebec H3A 1V8, Canada (tel: 514 842 5201); 120 Adelaide St West, Toronto, ON M5H 2EJ, Canada (tel: 416 363 2001).
> **Delta Airlines**, Hartsfield Atlanta International Airport, Atlanta, GA 39320, USA (tel: 404 765 5000).
> **Trans World Airlines**, 100 South Bedford Rd, Mount Kisco, NY 10549, USA (tel: 212 290 2141).
> **United Airlines**, PO Box 66100, O'Hare International Airport, Chicago, IL 60666, USA (tel: 312 952 4000).

For discount flights in North America try:

> **Access International**, 101 W 31st St, Suite 104, New York, NY 10010, USA (tel: 800/TAKE-OFF).
> **Council Travel**, 205 E 42nd St, New York, NY 10017, USA (tel: 212 661 1450). This is the head office of the nationwide student travel agents: there are branches in most big cities.
> **Nouvelles Frontières**, 12 E 33rd St, New York, NY 10016, USA (tel: 212 779 0600); 800 boulevard de Maisonneuve Est, Montréal, PQ H2L 4L8, Canada (tel: 514 288 9942). There are also offices in Los Angeles, San Francisco and Quebec City.
> **STA Travel**, 48 E 11th St, New York, NY 10003, USA (tel: 212 477 7166); 166 Geary St, Suite 702, San Francisco, CA 94108, USA

(tel: 415 391 8407). There are other offices in Los Angeles, Boston and Honolulu.

Travel Avenue, 180 N Jefferson, Chicago, IL 60606, USA (tel: 312 876 1116).

Travel Cuts, 187 College St, Toronto, ON M5T 1P7, Canada (tel: 416 979 2406). There are many other offices nationwide.

Maps and information

You can obtain free maps and information about your chosen area by dropping in at the Italian State Tourist Office (ENIT) in your country. Accommodation lists are available and they will be useful if you do not have anywhere to stay on immediate arrival. ENIT also issues a little book called the *Travellers' Handbook* which contains much useful information about Italy, not only for tourists but also for those who want to stay longer. ENIT offices overseas:

Australia/NZ: c/o Alitalia, AGC House, 124 Phillip St, Sydney, NSW.

Canada: 3 Place Ville Marie, 56 Plazaz, Montréal, Quebec H3B 2E3 (tel: 514 866 7667).

Eire: 47 Merrion Square, Dublin 2 (tel: 01 766397).

UK: 1 Princes Street, London W1R 8AY (tel: 071 408 1254).

USA: 630 Fifth Avenue, New York, NY 10111 (tel: 212 245 4822); 500 N Michigan Avenue, Chicago, IL 60611 (tel: 312 644 0990); 360 Post St, San Francisco, CA 94108 (tel: 415 392 6206).

Insurance

Getting some travel insurance before you go is strongly to be recommended, especially if you are outside the European Union. Try to get a policy which covers health as well, because no matter how organized you are it is unlikely that you will get your health situation in Italy sorted out inside of three months. You can ask about policies at travel agents and some banks. For UK nationals there is also Endsleigh Insurance (97 Southampton Row, London WC1B 4HH, tel: 081 436 4451) which offers cheap cover.

Passport/Visa

Check that your passport has not run out and that you have not lost it. This may seem obvious, but it often gets overlooked or left till the last minute. Remember, if you do not have a passport, it takes about a month to go through the whole procedure, even longer in busy periods.

Citizens of the UK, Ireland, the USA, Australia, New Zealand

and Canada do not need a visa to enter Italy. Of these, only the British and the Irish, however, are legally entitled to work there (EU membership entitles this). Nevertheless, once there they still have to go through various bureaucratic treadmills to get a *Permesso di Soggiorno* and *Libretto di Lavoro* (see Chapter 4).

For Australians, Americans, Canadians and New Zealanders, permission to visit Italy (for three months) does not entitle you to do anything except be a tourist. Many people come and start to work anyway, and there is little control on this practice. However, you are outside the law if you do so. To work legally you must have a work visa, and to get a work visa you have to submit a written promise of a job to the Italian Embassy in your country (see Chapter 4). The process is close to impossible and as a result there are very few non-European English teachers who are working legally in Italy.

Books

All good travel bookshops have a wide selection of material on Italy, from studies of art and culture to straightforward travel guides. Best to get these before you go, as you may not have access to an English-language bookshop when you arrive – and, even if you do, the range will be smaller and the prices higher. A list of recommended publications is given in Appendix 7.

Italian language and culture

Italian is not a difficult language to learn, especially if you already have some experience of language learning. If you have time, make the effort to learn some Italian – it will make your entry into life in Italy much easier. Evening classes or teach-yourself books are both good solutions (see Appendix 7 for a list of recommended books).

For information concerning legal or cultural matters, contact the Italian Embassy in your country. If they cannot help you themselves they will be able to put you in touch with someone who can:

> *Australia*: Embassy of Italy, 12 Grey St, Deakin, ACT 2000, Canberra (tel: 06 733333).
>
> *Canada*: Italian Consulate, 3489 Drummond St, Quebec H3G 1X6 (tel: 514 849 8351); or 275 Slater St, 11th Floor, Ottawa, Ontario K1P 5H9 (tel: 613 232 2402).
>
> *New Zealand*: Embassy of Italy, 34 Grant Road, Wellington (tel: 04 735339).
>
> *UK*: Embassy of Italy, 2 Melville Crescent, Edinburgh (tel: 031 226 3631); or 38 Eaton Place, London SW1X 8AN (tel: 071 235 9371).

USA: Embassy of Italy, 690 Park Avenue, New York, NY 10221-5044 (tel: 212 737 9100); or 500 N Michigan Avenue, Suite 1850, Chicago, IL (tel: 312 467 1550) or 1300 Post Cak Boulevard, Suite 660, Houston, TX (tel: 713 850 7520); or 2590 Webster St, San Francisco, CA (tel: 415 931 4924); or 100 Boylston St, Suite 900, Boston, MA (tel: 617 542 0483); or 12400 Wilsaire Boulevard, Los Angeles, CA (tel: 213 820 0622).

WHAT TO TAKE

Going to live in Italy will not deprive you of anything very serious – baked beans, instant coffee and fish and chip shops are the only things people seem to miss. If you are really desperate for some 'genuine food' from the homeland, foreign foods can be found in the smart and expensive delicatessen-type shops which are popping up in almost every city.

There are, however, a few practical things which old-hands always recommend to people coming to teach in Italy, and these are listed below.

All your official documents. Take your birth certificate, educational qualifications, driving licence (try to make it international before you leave), Youth Hostel membership card, and anything else that looks official. Italian bureaucracy loves documents, so the more the better. An authenticated translation of your degree certificate helps a lot when you are trying to get a job. You can get this done at the Italian Embassy at home for a modest fee.

Several passport-size photos. It is worth spending a little more and getting them done by a professional photographer as you will have to live with the photos on all your documents for a long time.

Some smart clothes. Men should have at least a tie and white shirt available, if only for the job-hunt stage.

Money. The amount you will need to take with you will depend on whether or not you are going to a pre-arranged job, and whether you are going to be put up by someone for the initial period. Bear in mind that setting up home in a shared flat will cost you about a million lire, and not all schools are willing to help you out on this. If you are going without a job and intending to sleep in *pensioni* to start with, you will need about two million lire to see you through the period between arrival and getting a regular income. Travellers' cheques are a handy alternative to carrying wads of cash around.

Realia. This is TEFL-speak for anything from home that has English written on it – eg brochures, newspapers, theatre programmes, a corn-flakes packet. Anything visibly real is far more interesting to students than what is in their textbook. With a little imagination you can organize whole lessons around the label on a tin of beans.

A kettle. Not strictly necessary, but the fact that electric kettles are very hard to come by in Italy has been known to cause distress.

Part 2

LIVING IN ITALY

6 │ Arriving and everyday living

This chapter deals with some essential aspects of living in Italy. First, however, you have to get to where you're going.

TRANSPORT FROM THE AIRPORT

Rome

Charter flights arrive at Ciampino airport, while the bigger Fiumicino handles scheduled flights. Don't even think about getting a taxi. From Fiumicino there is a special train which runs roughly every half hour from inside the airport to the air terminal at Ostiense. Once there, look for the metro (big white M on red background) and head for the centre (*direzione Rebibbia/ Termini*).

From Ciampino take the only orange bus that comes to the airport (you buy tickets from the airport newsagent) and get off at Anagnina metro station. From there take a train (*direzione Termini/Ottaviano*) to the centre.

Milan

Milan has two airports, Linante and Malpensa. If you arrive at Linante, there is a special bus which will take you the 7 km to the city centre in about 20 minutes. It costs 3500 lire and buses leave every 20 minutes. The bus sets you down at Piazza Luigi di Savoia, near the central station.

Malpensa airport, which tends to handle intercontinental flights, is 50 km outside Milan. There are buses direct to the central station (about one hour) or to the air terminal at Lampugnamo station on the M1 metro line (35 minutes).

Naples

Capodichino Airport is connected to Piazza Garibaldi in the centre of Naples by bus No 14 which passes every 15 minutes or so. Buy

33

the tickets from the tobacconist inside the airport. There is also an official airport bus, but it is more expensive, passes less frequently, and is no quicker. Taking a taxi should cost in the region of 30 000 lire.

URGENT ACCOMMODATION

Rome

Rome has an abundance of cheap places to stay, and even in the height of summer you should be able to find something suitable. Even so, prior booking is better. There are several hostels:

> **Ostello del Foro Italico**, Viale delle Olimpiadi 61 (tel: 06 3236279). Somewhat out of the centre. Metro to Ottaviano, then bus No 32.
> **Ottaviano**, Via Ottaviano 6 (tel: 06 383956). Metro to Ottaviano.
> **Pensionato Concezioniste di Lourdes**, Via Sistina 113 (tel: 06 4745324). This is a convent, and for women only. Metro Spagna.
> **Raccuia**, Via Treviso 37 (tel: 06 8831406). Metro Policlinico.
> **Sandy**, Via Cavour 136 (tel: 06 483121). Metro Cavour.
> **Villa Santa Cecilia**, Via Argeleto 54 (tel: 06 52371688). Metro Magliana.

Many of the city's cheap hotels and *pensioni* are around Termini Station. The following are cheap and trustworthy, if not exactly luxurious. Unless stated they are within easy walking distance of the station:

> **Cervia**, Via Palestro 55 (tel: 06 491057).
> **Eureka**, Piazza della Republica 47 (tel: 06 4825806).
> **Gexim**, Via Palestro 34 (tel: 06 4460211).
> **Liberiano**, Via S Prassede 25 (tel: 06 4828804).
> **Mari**, Via Palestro 55 (tel: 06 4462137).
> **Mari II**, Via Calatafimi 38 (tel: 06 4740371).
> **Marsala**, Via Marsala 36 (tel: 06 4456861).
> **Perugia**, Via del Colosseo 7 (tel: 06 6797200).
> **Romano**, Largo C Ricci 32 (tel: 06 6795851). Metro Cavour.
> **Tony**, Via P Amadeo 79d (tel: 06 4466887).

Milan

Accommodation tends to be expensive in this city, but you will find most of the cheaper hotels and *pensioni* around the station (naturally), Corso Buenos Aires and Piazzale Loreto. There is one hostel:

Ostello Piero Rotta, Via Martino Bassi 2 (tel: 02 39267095). Open 7–9 am and 5–11 pm. M1 metro to Lotto. It is best to book in advance.

Your only other option is one of the cheaper hotels. Here are a few:

Arno, Via Lazzaretto 17 (tel: 02 6705509). Tram No 4 or 11.
Arthur, Via Lazzaretto 14 (tel: 02 2046294). Tram as above.
Canna, Viale Tunisia 6 (tel: 02 2952219). Central.
San Tommaso, Viale Tunisia 6 (tel: 02 29514747). Central.
Siena, Via P Castaldi 17 (tel: 02 29514615). Central.
Villa Mira, Via Sacchini 19 (tel: 02 2041618). Near Piazzale Loreto.

Naples

As usual the cheapest hotel accommodation is near the station. The city gets pretty crowded with tourists in the summer, so book ahead if you can. Don't take any notice of the characters at the station who offer to take you to a hotel. The official youth hostel in Naples is very cheap, although not in the centre:

Ostello Mergellina, Salita della Grotta 23 (tel: 081 7612346). Metro to Mergellina or bus No 152 from Piazza Garibaldi in front of the station.

Some safe and not too expensive hotels are (near the station unless stated):

Ambra, Via Mezzacanone 109 (tel: 081 5529256). Near University.
Casanova, Via Venezia 2 (tel: 081 268287).
Crispi, Via Crispi 104 (tel: 081 668048). Metro Mergellina.
Ginevra, Via Genova 116 (tel: 081 283210).
Imperia, Piazza Luigi Miraglia 386 (tel: 081 459347). Near Piazza Dante.
Odeon, Via Silvio Spaventa (tel: 081 285656).
San Pietro, San Pietro ad Aram 18 (tel: 081 5535914).

INFORMATION

Rome

There are Tourist Offices (generally open Monday–Saturday, 8 am–7 pm) at Termini Station, at Fiumicino Airport, and at Via Parigi 5 (5 minutes walk from Termini). Here they have maps and other information about the city. Also try the 'Enjoy Rome' office in Via Varese 39, which has a free room-finding service.

Milan

Try the Tourist Information offices, one of which is in the central station (open Monday–Saturday, 8 am–7 pm) and the other is at Via Marconi 1 on the corner of Piazza Duomo (open Monday–Saturday, 8 am–8 pm; Sunday, 9 am–5 pm).

Naples

There are tourist offices at the airport (Monday–Friday, 8 am–2 pm and 5 pm–7 pm), at Mergellina station (times as for the airport office), at Piazza Gesù Nuovo (Monday–Saturday, 9 am–7 pm; Sunday, 9 am–3 pm) and at the central station (Monday–Saturday, 9 am–7 pm; Sunday, 9 am–3 pm). They all issue maps and can point you towards some decent accommodation.

BANKS AND MONEY MATTERS

Banks

Banks in Italy are uniformly bad news. It is difficult to spend any time in them without feeling angry and upset. The reasons for this are basically twofold. First, most banks are state-owned, so their employees have jobs from which they cannot be sacked. Second, jobs in banks, and especially higher-level ones, are given out for political reasons rather than professional competence. This explains much of the arrogance and incompetence you will see there. To work in a bank is the ambition of many a young Italian. It is secure, widely respected and you work relatively short hours.

Practical information

Bank opening times are: 9 am–1 pm and 2.30 pm–3.30 pm. Credit cards are only just beginning to be widely used, but even so you cannot rely on them for everyday living – many places will not have anything to do with them. Cheques too are usually limited to the transference of large sums of money between people who trust each other (or who know that the other person is still going to be around next week). A word of warning about cheques: unless they have *non transferibile* stamped on them, they can be cashed by anyone – and that includes anyone who manages to steal them from you.

Another problem is that if you pay cheques into an account, they take at least a week to clear. Obviously this can be very inconvenient if you want to use the money immediately. Automatic cash tills (*Bancomat*) are becoming more common now after a slow start, and if your bank at home will issue you a Eurocheque card, this is a good way to have access to money in an emergency.

If you cannot get hold of a Eurocheque card, you are advised to bring either a credit card (American Express or Visa are the most widely accepted) or a stack of travellers' cheques. Either of these should enable you to get your hands on cash quickly if disaster strikes.

Transferring money from/to home

If you have a bank account here this is very easy. Just give your bank the details of where you want the money to go and for a charge of 10 000 lire they will sort it all out for you. The same applies for anyone back home who wants to send you money.

If you do not have an account it is trickier, but still possible. Get someone at home to telex a draft to the Banca d'Italia or Banca Nazionale del Lavoro nearest to you (local banks can organize this). Make sure that the telex includes details of your passport number. The process can take up to four days and obviously you will have to prove your identity when you go to pick the money up.

Opening an account

To open a bank account you need to take your *Permesso di Soggiorno*, your passport and your *Codice Fiscale* to the bank of your choice and ask to open a *conto corrente* (current account). Some banks also ask for a letter from your employer stating that you are employed and receiving a salary of so many lire every month.

If you have all the necessay documents you can open an account in a morning. You will be issued with a book of cheques and that is about it. Cheque guarantee cards do not exist because nobody trusts them and service-till cards are very rarely issued to foreigners, presumably because nobody trusts them either.

At time of writing bank charges are 2 300 lire per operation, 10 000 for a statement and 35 000 at the end of each fiscal year.

Money

Italian banknotes come with so many noughts on them that it is easy to get confused. Unscrupulous taxi-drivers and shop-assistants have been known to take advantage of this, so double-check every time you pay for anything. Banknotes come in denominations of 100 000, 50 000, 10 000, 5 000, 2 000 and 1 000, while coins are 500, 200, 100, 50 (there are still a few at 20 and 10 knocking about, but these are so little that they're hardly worth keeping).

There are also telephone tokens which serve as money. They are worth 200 lire. At time of writing, exchange rates (in lire) are approximately: US dollar – 1606; UK sterling – 2438; Irish pound – 2387; Canadian dollar – 1158; and Australian dollar – 1179.

COST OF LIVING

People who visited Italy 30 years ago will probably tell you that it is a very cheap place to live. It was. Now it is not – at least not in the big cities. You can have a good standard of living in Italy – everything you need is freely available – but don't expect to save much money while you are here. Also remember that the cost of living is substantially less in the south than in the north.

A reasonable monthly salary for an English teacher is about 1.6 million lire net. With this much in your hand at the end of every month you can live quite comfortably. Remember, however, that if you get that much at the end of the month, with all your contributions and tax paid, your actual gross earnings are more like 3 million, given the costs of staying *in regola* (within the law). If you avoid paying everything except the 19% *Ritenuta d'acconto* (see p 22) it should be reasonably easy to arrive at 1.6 million.

Accommodation will cost you anything from 400 000 to 600 000 lire if you share a flat, considerably more if you want to live on your own. This leaves you with about a million to eat, drink and be merry with.

Eating and drinking

The meanest person I know reckons to spend 35 000 a week on food and drink. He goes to the supermarket and buys only the bare essentials to keep body and soul together. I buy food at the shops near my house (generally more expensive than markets and supermarkets) and I spend about 50 000 or 60 000.

Eating out (a pizza, a beer and an ice-cream) generally comes to about 20 000 or 25 000 a head, so you can do it a few times per week, but no more.

Being merry . . .

Going to discothèques and night clubs is a big drain. They start at about 15 000 admission and the drinks once you are inside are pretty expensive. Cinema costs 10 000; 3 drinks in a trendy bar will come to about 20 000; and an ice-cream costs about 2 000.

Table 1. Comparative living expenses (thousands of lire).

	Rome	Madrid	London	Paris
Veal fillet (1 kg)	35	15	24	55
Monthly rent of 100 m² flat in centre	2 900	1 200	1 400	3 300
Taxi – basic fare	6	1.7	2.2	2.5
Labourer's annual salary	17 900	19 500	19 400	17 650
Clothing (sweater)	145	105	135	200
Compact disc	25	21.6	30	29.6
Microwave oven	290	275	260	220
Theatre	33	12	55	33

Source: La Stampa, January 1993.

Here is a list of international products so that you can compare with prices at home (prices in lire):

> Can of Coke – 1 500
> Packet of 20 Marlboro – 4 250
> Cheap bottle of wine – 4 000
> TDK C-90 cassette – 3 000
> KitKat chocolate bar – 1 000
> Daily newspaper – 1 200
> Kellogg's Corn Flakes – 4 250
> Litre of milk – 1 750
> Any journey on the metro – 1 000

Table 1 is a comparative price list published by *La Stampa* in January 1993. Rome is a good sample to take because its prices are average for Italy. Further south you may pay less, and in the north you generally pay more.

COMMUNICATIONS

Post

There seems to be very little consistency in the service provided by the Italian Post Office. At times it can function quite normally, at others it is hopelessly slow and sometimes letters/parcels simply go missing (to be fair the service is better than it was and this happens much less frequently than it did).

To avoid delays and to feel relatively secure, there are three other ways you can send letters which seem to be more reliable. Naturally they cost more. They are airmail (*via aeria*), express (*espresso*) and registered (*raccommandata*). These last two take just as long as ordinary postage, so don't be fooled into thinking you are paying for speed as well as security. If you want to speed things up, posting letters at the nearest railway station might take a day or two off journey time.

Although you can buy stamps (*francobolli*) at tobacconists, you can never be sure that they really know how much each postage category costs, so it is safer to do it all at the *Posta*. Post offices always have yellow signs outside with 'PT' on them. Rates and average postage times for normal weight letters are:

> to UK – 750 lire, 5–6 days
> to North America – 1 250 lire, 7–10 days
> to Australia/NZ – 1 350 lire, 10 days

Espresso letters cost 3 750 lire within Europe, and 3 850 outside. *Raccommandata* costs 3 950 lire within Europe and 4 050 outside.

Postcards cost 700 lire, but they are low-priority mail so they can take anything up to a month to arrive.

If you do not have a fixed address and need to receive mail, arrange to have it sent to the Post Office in your town (if it is a big town, make sure you get the right Post Office). The writer needs to write your surname very clearly and put *fermo posta* next to it. When you pick it up you may have to prove your identity.

Telephones

Public telephones are to be found in some bars, in booths on the street, and often in stations there is a SIP (national telephone company) telephone office where you can go to make a call and then pay afterwards at the desk.

The minimum fee for a call is 200 lire, and phones usually take coins of 100, 200, and 500 lire as well as the special tokens (*gettoni*) which are worth 200 lire. There are also many with a phone-card facility. Phone-cards can be bought at most tobacconists (look for a white 'T' on a black sign) for 5 000 or 10 000 lire. If you are making international calls, they are much more convenient.

With regard to private telephones, if your flat does not have a phone, to get one you will have to contact the local SIP office and ask to have one installed. It will cost about 340 000 lire.

To make international calls dial 00, then the country code (America and Canada – 1, UK – 44, Australia – 61 and New Zealand – 64), then the area code and then the number. If the area code begins with a zero, it is usually dropped. If you want to make a call reversing the charges, ask the operator for *contassa al carico del destinatario*.

Telephone talk	
Hello?	*Pronto?*
Can I speak to . . .	*Posso parlare con . . .*
(S)he's not in	*Non c'è*
I'll call back later	*Richiamerò più tardi*
When will (s)he be back?	*Quando tornerà?*

The cheapest time to make phone calls is between 2.30 pm on Saturday and 8 am on Monday. Avoid the top-rate on weekday mornings.

Codes for major Italian cities

If you are calling Italy from abroad dial 01039, then the code below, followed by the number. If you are calling inside Italy, put a zero in front of the city code.

Bari	80	Naples	81
Bologna	51	Palermo	91
Florence	55	Rome	6
Genoa	10	Turin	11
Milan	2	Venice	41

Telegraph

The safest (and quickest) way to send a message over long distances is with the telegraph service. Post Offices will send telegrams for you at a rate of about 800 lire per word.

ACCOMMODATION

This section is divided into two parts: short-term and long-term accommodation. The first will probably be useful when you first arrive, and also later when you go travelling around. The second part deals mainly with the difficult business of finding a flat or a house.

Short-term

Many people who come to Italy to teach arrive with the address of a friend where they can stay till they sort out a place for themselves. Obviously this is the ideal solution, because you are saved the expense of a *pensione* and you have access to useful information.

Other people arrive with no reference point whatsoever, check into a cheap *pensione* and stay there until their situation stabilizes. This solution is perfectly workable, as long as you have the money to pay for two or three weeks' accommodation before you start earning. On the whole a *pensione* is a better option than a youth hostel at this stage because it will give you some privacy and the chance to prepare lessons in peace if you start teaching before you find a fixed abode.

It is also worth checking the noticeboards in the English bookshops (see below). People often want to let their rooms for short periods while they go away on holiday, so if you find something available it will give you welcome time and space to sort out the rest of your immediate problems.

If you arrive in one of the big cities with nowhere to go, stow your luggage at the railway station and head for the tourist information office. This may be in the station itself, but if not it will be signposted. There they should give you a list of hotels and *pensioni* and a map of the town. Find the ones within your price range and go round there at once – they fill up quickly in the summer months.

Another place worth visiting is the local *Centro Turistico Studentesco* (CTS) office. This is a young people's travel organization with offices in most major towns and cities. They are very good at helping you find and book accommodation in *pensioni* and dormitories and they are sure to know the cheapest options. Addresses for some main cities are:

> *Florence*: Via dei Ginori, 25/R (tel: 055 289721).
> *Rome*: Via Genova, 16 (tel: 06 46791).
> *Milan*: Via S Antonio, 2 (tel: 02 58304121).
> *Naples*: Via Mezzocannone, 25 (tel: 081 5527975).
> *Turin*: Via Camerana, 3/E (tel: 011 534388).

Hotels (Alberghi)

There is a very wide range of hotel accommodation available all over Italy. While there are no longer any incredibly cheap places, there are many that offer simple services for a reasonable price. If you are looking for a place just for yourself, remember that many establishments have very few single rooms and, when they do, they cost about two-thirds as much as a double.

At the bottom of the market are *locande*, something like inns, which are found off rather than on the beaten track and more in the south than in the north. Expect to pay about 25 000 lire for a double room without bath/shower.

Next up the scale is the *pensione* which simply means a small, cheaper hotel. They are sometimes classed as one-star hotels and offer what you would expect in that class – essential, no-frills accommodation. Here you will pay between 30 000 and 40 000 for a double, more for one with a shower/bath.

After this you are out of the cheap end and into well-off tourist country. Two-star hotels cost upwards of 50 000 lire, less if they offer rooms without showers (not all do). You probably will not see much difference between these and a reasonable *pensione*. Anything above this and you will see a difference, but then you will be paying 70 000–80 000 at the very least.

Prices vary considerably according to the season and also to the location, but in one town on one day you are unlikely to make much of a saving by shopping around. Also, be careful about getting stung for meals – they often try to include breakfast in the cost and sometimes other meals as well. You can always eat cheaper elsewhere so, unless you do not mind paying for the convenience, insist on a room-only deal – before, not after, you accept the room.

For the cheapest accommodation in any town or city, take a look round the railway station. What you find may not be very salubrious but it will be the cheapest hotel accommodation available (20 000 lire is about as low as you get for a single room).

Hotel talk	
single	*camera singola*
with a double bed	*camera matrimoniale*
with two single beds	*camera doppia*
room for 3/4/5 . . . people	*camera per 3/4/5 . . .*
with/without shower/bathroom	*con/senza doccia/bagno*

For a list of hotels and prices in your town go to the local tourist office (*Ente Provinciale Turismo* – EPT) and ask for the *annuario alberghi*. This is a free booklet listing all the hotels in the area, together with prices and facilities. There are also explanations in English.

Hostels

The good points about youth hostels are that they are cheap (about 12 000 lire a night), you can meet a lot of people, and they are often in very beautiful places. The bad points are that they tend to be inconvenient for town centres, and you are locked out during the day and have to be in by a certain time at night. Also, you have no privacy as you sleep in a dormitory with six or seven other people.

There are about 50 youth hostels in Italy and they are all members of the International Youth Hostel Federation (IYHF) so if you already have a IYHF card you can use them straight away. If you do not have one, you can usually become a member on the spot, or else pay a little more for accommodation.

If you want information on this before you go, contact the following:

> *US*: American Youth Hostels, PO Box 37613, Washington, DC 20013-7613 (tel: 202 783 6161).
>
> *Canada*: Canadian Hostelling Association, 1600 James Naismith Drive, Gloucester, Ontario K1B 5N4 (tel: 613 748 5638).
>
> *UK*: Youth Hostel Association, Trevelyan House, 8 St Stephen's Hill, St Albans, Herts AL1 2DY (tel: 0727 55215).
>
> *Australia*: Australian Youth Hostel Association, 60 Mary St, Surry Hills, Sydney, NSW 2010 (tel: 02 212 1151).
>
> *New Zealand*: Youth Hostels Association of New Zealand, PO Box 436, Corner of Manchester and Gloucester St, Christchurch 1 (tel: 03 799970).

For information when you are in Italy, either look through the local phone book for *Associazione Italiana Alberghi per la Gioventù* (AIG), or contact their headquarters in Rome: **AIG**, Via Cavour 44, 00184 Rome (tel: 06 462342); or **AIG**, Palazzo della Civiltà del Lavoro, Quadrato della Concordia, 00144 Rome–EUR (tel: 06 462342).

Long-term

Finding flats in Italian cities is hard. However, as a foreigner you have an advantage because many landlords will prefer you to an Italian. It is assumed that you will go away sooner and that you will not make a fuss if they ask you to leave. This belief has come about thanks to tenancy laws which protect local residents from being thrown out of rented accommodation at short notice. For this reason many landlords specify *non-residenti* or *uso foresteria* (foreigners) in their adverts. Most foreigners, at least initially, live in shared apartments. Living alone is generally prohibited by the lack of small apartments with rents that one person could reasonably afford. If you are intent on living alone, look for ads for *monolocale*, or *appartamentino*. These are small flats designed for one person, and are few and far between.

Especially in cities, there seems to be an abundance of 3-roomed apartments for around 1.5 million per month. The obvious solution then is to share.

Prices

For a room in a shared flat in the main cities, 500 000 lire is about average. To get a place on your own you will have to pay at least 800 000 lire. In smaller centres expect to pay somewhat less. To move in, you will often be asked to pay two months' rent in advance plus, sometimes, a deposit which will be the equivalent of a month's rent.

Other costs

Apart from the rent you will have to pay *condominio*. This is a contribution to the cost of maintaining and cleaning the *palazzo* (block) in which you have your flat. Sometimes the landlord includes this in the rent.

There is also the *riscaldamento* (central heating) to pay, although sometimes it is in included in the *condominio*. The amount you pay will depend on the number of radiators in your flat, and usually you have no control over how much you use them because they are controlled centrally and switched on at times established at the *riunione di condominio* (tenants' meeting).

Other bills, like gas, electricity, water and telephone will arrive in your letter box at regular intervals and it is obviously up to you to pay them before you get cut off. You do this by tearing off the bottom part of the bill and taking it to the nearest post office with the money.

All these extra costs vary enormously and so it pays to find out as much as you can before you take a place on. Ask for details of *condominio*, *riscaldamento* and how much the other bills total.

Flats – general information

The majority of Italians live in flats in apartment-blocks, and it is very likely that you will end up in something similar. These *palazzi*

> I had just moved into a rented flat in a small town where I had found work for the summer. One lunchtime I invited a female colleague to come and see it and have something to eat with me. About five minutes after we got there my landlord arrived and took me aside saying that I wasn't to bring *donne* into the flat. Apparently the neighbours would start talking.
>
> *Richard Hayes (New Zealand)*

are very rarely anything to look at but they provide efficient, affordable housing for millions of people in cities where having a 'house' in the British or American sense is financially out of the question. Generally they have two or three staircases, unsurprisingly called *scala A, scala B*, etc, and this is important when giving your address, or taking someone else's. *Palazzi* often have a concierge (*portiere*) who sits in a little glass-fronted box and sullenly watches everybody who comes in and out.

Flats nearly always have a balcony, or a terrace of sorts, and the value of this is not to be underestimated. The climate is good enough for this outside space to serve as another room for much of the year. Baths are not common; showers are universal; and the toilet is always in the bathroom. Plug sockets are the same two-pin variety to be found in much of Europe and the power supply is 220 volts.

Carpets and curtains are the exception rather than the rule. Floors are usually tiled because tiles are cooler in the summer and because carpets are seen as rather unhygienic. Curtains are not necessary as windows usually have French-style shutters (*serrande*) or Venetian blinds (*persiane*).

Flat descriptions in newspapers and elsewhere can take some deciphering. A typical advert looks like this:

> *Colosseo camera ammobiliato in appmto 100 mq 500 000 tel.786543 ore pasti e serali*

or this:

> *Appio-Latino foresteria signorile tre camere balconi servizi box auto 1.700 000 tel. 456987*

The first of these is offering a furnished (*ammobiliato*) room in a shared apartment of 100 square metres near the Colosseum. The rent is 500 000 lire a month, and you are to ring up at mealtimes (*ore pasti*) or in the evening (*serali*).

The second is a complete flat in the Appio-Latino area. It is for foreigners only (*foresteria*), considers itself a bit posh (*signorile*), has got three rooms which could be bedrooms, living room or anything you want, and has got a kitchen and bathroom (*servizi*). *Box Auto* means a garage for your car and 1.7 million is the monthly rent.

As you can see from these examples, the adverts give very little information. Sometimes they do not even tell you the price (a bad sign). Save all your questions about bills and *condominio* till you are face-to-face with the landlord.

Where to look for a flat

University noticeboards. If your town or city has a university, there will be at least one noticeboard with rooms and flats for rent. Whatever the prices are here, you can take as a measure of the cheap end of the market. Usually they will be single rooms on offer, in flats which you share with other people. Sometimes students share rooms, so check that it says *camera* or *stanza* (room) and not *posto letto* (bed).

English-language bookstore. Every large city has one and it usually contains a noticeboard used by the English-speaking community to find and rent accommodation. The added advantage is that the adverts will probably be in English. You can leave a message too, if you have a contact phone number. For example:

> *Rome*: **The Economy Bookstore**, Via Torino; **The Lion Bookshop**, Via del Babuino.
> *Milan*: **The English Bookshop**, Via Ariosto.
> *Turin*: **Susan's Bookshop**, VS Quintino, 8.
> *Florence*: **BM Bookshop**, Borgo Ognissanti, 4/r.
> *Naples*: **Universal Books**, Rione Sirignano, 1.

English-language newspapers. English newspapers such as *Wanted in Rome* have regular accommodation pages and will always be available in the bookshops mentioned above. Often the rents asked in these are ridiculously high because they are aimed at embassy staff and the employees of other government organizations that are assumed to be rolling in money. However, every now and then you can find reasonable offers, and in these cases it is often the first person to answer the advert who gets the place. Getting hold of the papers and telephoning as soon as they come out are therefore essential.

Italian local newspapers. Every city has an *Exchange & Mart* type newspaper, available in kiosks, in which there is a section called *Appartamenti in Affitto*. As before, get the paper and get phoning as soon as you can. Here are a few of the better-known papers of this type:

> *Rome*: *Porta Portese*
> *Milan*: *Seconda Mano*
> *Naples*: *Bric-a-brac* or *Fiera Città*
> *Florence*: *La Pulce*
> *Turin*: *Torino Affari*

These newspapers are also good for getting furniture and other household equipment like washing machines, cookers and fridges very cheaply. You can put an ad in yourself (it is usually free), stating what you want and giving your telephone number, or you can scour the pages for what you want and then ring up the number if you find it. There is also a section called *in regalo* which is full of things that people are trying to get rid of, and therefore will let you have for nothing if you go and collect them.

Agencies. Flat-finding agencies are an easy option if you have the money. They will usually find you a place fairly quickly, and let you see a few before you decide. Unfortunately, for their services they will charge you at least the equivalent of one month's rent in the property you eventually accept. They advertise themselves everywhere so you should not have difficulty finding one, but, if you do, look in the yellow pages under *Agenzie Immobiliari* and find one that says *affitti* (renting).

Affittasi signs. Many landlords put up fluorescent green or orange signs on the wall of the *palazzo* where they have a flat to rent. These signs will have *affittasi* (to let) written on them in large letters followed by a few details of the flat and a telephone number. Check that it does not say *uso ufficio* (for use as an office).

Portieri. If you are really keen, and you speak enough Italian, you could go round all the *palazzi* in an area you like, asking the *portieri* (concierges) if they know of any empty, or soon to be empty apartments in the block. It takes a lot of time, and you have no guarantee of success, but if you do find something you will be at an immediate advantage because probably only you will know about it.

HEALTH

If you become ill, and you do not already have a doctor, you should go to the *pronto soccorso* (casualty) or *ambulatorio* (general surgery) of the nearest hospital. If it is really serious, ring 113 and ask for *ospedale* or *ambulanza*.

For minor ailments it is probably better to go to the local *farmacia* (chemist/pharmacist). They are usually very helpful, they know what they are talking about, and they can sell you the necessary medicines right away. Most towns have at least one open all night – to find it go to any *farmacia* and look at the notice on the door which tells you where the nearest all-night service is. Alternatively look in the daily paper, in the *Informazioni Utili* section.

Dentistry

Theoretically, dental treatment is paid for by the USL (state health care) but the system is so slow and inconvenient that most Italians go private. This is very expensive, and it is much better to get regular checks done at home (if you go back often enough), leaving Italian dentists for emergency cases. This is not because they are bad (Italian dentistry is considered among the best in the world), but simply because of the cost.

EU citizens

As an EU citizen you are entitled to free medical treatment in *ospedale* (hospitals) and *ambulatorio* (surgeries). At the beginning of their stay, UK nationals can use the E111 form (available at DSS offices in the UK) to prove entitlement, but this does not last forever and after about six months you are expected to be registered with a doctor in Italy. To do this, you need to go to your local USL (*Unità Sanitaria Locale*) office with all your documents plus proof that you are paying state health/insurance contributions – either a letter from your school or two *buste paga* (wage slips). The USL will give you a medical health number and let you choose a doctor from their local list.

Once you have a doctor, then all the medicine and tests he/she prescribes will be covered by the *mutuo* (state subsidy for health care) and you should end up paying about 10% of the full cost.

Non-EU citzens

The law in this area changes frequently but the situation at time of writing is as follows. If you are not an EU citizen and you do not have a work visa, then you do not have very many rights. You are, in effect, a tourist and you will receive hospital treatment in an emergency but you will be expected to pay for it at a later date (this does not include Australians, whose country has a bilateral agreement with the Italian government). You have no right to a doctor and you will have to pay the full price of any medicines, tests and analyses.

If you have a work visa, then you will have all the necessary documentation to receive your share of state health care. At this point your position becomes identical to that of an EU citizen (see above).

Medical assistance for freelance teachers

If you are working on your own, or for a school that does not pay national health contributions, you can still obtain medical assistance. To do this, you have to go to the USL, with your *Residenza*, declare yourself freelance (*libera professionista*) and pay a minimum of 750 000 lire for one year. This payment substitutes what you would have paid in contributions, had you been working for someone on contract.

The address of your nearest USL office can be found in the front of *Tutto Città* (the free city map-book distributed by the phone company) or in the phone-book itself. There is one for each district of a city, so be sure to go to the right one for your area.

TRANSPORT

Rail

Trains in Italy are relatively cheap, thanks to the heavy government subsidies which FS (*Ferrovia dello Stato*) receives. The service is not renowned for its punctuality, but this is not its greatest defect. That honour goes to the desperate overcrowding that can make a journey in the summer months seem like hell. This varies, of course, according to when you travel and what type of train you take.

If you have any choice at all, try not to travel at weekends (including late Friday and early Monday) or on public holidays (see Appendix 6). Generally the summer months are ghastly all the way through because of the heat and the mish-mash of foreign backpackers, holidaying Italians and shady characters out to rip you off in one way or another.

The different types of train are:

- *Rapido*. These are fast, air-conditioned and quite comfortable. They are more expensive than other types, but still not that much more than normal trains elsewhere in Europe. You often have to book your seat several hours in advance; it will say *prenotazione obligatorio* on the timetable if this is the case.

- *Eurocity/Intercity*. These are the same as the *Rapidi* except that Eurocities sometimes go to destinations outside Italy. Why it is necessary to have three names for the same thing is a mysteiy. Italian Railway's pride and joy is the Eurocity *Pendolino* (Pendulum) which rushes backwards and forwards between Rome and Milan. Needless to say the *Pendolino* is chic and very expensive.
- *Espresso*. Probably the most common type, inexpensive and hence frequently packed. There seems to be no limit to numbers so you can find yourself standing in a space the size of your feet for the whole journey. On the other hand, if you get a seat and there are not too many people breathing down your neck travelling by the *Espresso* can be quite comfortable and even pleasant.
- *Diretto*. Do not be taken in by the name. They stop at every little station for an excruciating amount of time and while you may well have space to relax in (they are rarely full) you will probably go mad with boredom before you reach your destination.
- *Locale*. As for *Diretto*.

Getting tickets

When possible try to get tickets before you are due to travel. Train tickets can be bought at authorized travel agents in most cities, and it is much less trouble than at the station where, in big cities like Rome and Milan, queues tend to get very long. Give yourself at least 30 minutes to be sure of not missing your train. Some places are also equipped with ticket machines of the tap-the-screen variety. These are very useful when they work, but the queues for them can get long too and they are rather temperamental about accepting crumpled paper money.

If you use the train a lot and are under 26, get yourself a *Carta Verde* (Green Card), which will give you a discount on train tickets. It costs around 10 000 lire.

Prices of some common train journeys			
(standard second-class single in lire)			
Rome–Milan	43 000	Milan–Turin	12 000
Rome–Venice	40 000	Milan–Bologna	15 000
Rome–Palermo	63 000	Milan–Verona	11 000
Rome–Naples	15 000	Milan–Bari	60 000

Buses and trams

Buses and trams are usually run by the same people, so tickets for one are valid on the other. The service provided is generally pretty good, considering the amount of traffic on the roads. As with the trains, overcrowding can be a problem, not only because it is uncomfortable, but also because pickpockets take advantage of the press of bodies to fleece you.

The service usually shuts down by midnight, if not before, and the night service, which does not exist in some cities, is infrequent at the best of times.

Bus and tram stops generally have a list of street names and *piazzas* under each line number, which is fine if you know the city but pretty useless if you do not. Either take a map with you, or better still get a bus/tram route map – available at most news kiosks. Alternatively there is usually someone around to give you a hand if you can understand them.

Getting tickets

You have to buy tickets before you get on board from a *Tabacchi* (tobacconist shop – look for a big white 'T' on a black back-ground), certain news kiosks, or from the little ticket booths which you see at the more important termini. Once on the bus you have to stamp your ticket in the dramatic sounding *obliteratrice*, other-wise it is not valid.

Each town operates a slightly different ticket system, but usually one journey costs about 1 200 lire. Some cities, like Rome, have 90-minute tickets with which you can go anywhere, and on any number of buses within the time limit. Given the traffic, it is not always the bargain you might imagine.

If you use them frequently, you can get an *abbonamento* (season ticket) for buses, trams and the metro too. They cost about 37 000 lire a month.

Coaches

For longer-distance journeys, a viable alternative to the trains are coaches. They cost about the same as trains, and surprisingly are often quicker, as they take full advantage of the good network of *autostrade*. They also go to many places that trains do not, so they may be your only option. Naturally they are subject to traffic problems, so you can never rely on them to get you somewhere for a certain time. They can also be hot and uncomfortable.

Despite the fact that they are run by private companies they always seem to be blue, and so too are the coach stops. Generally the *capolinea* (terminus) is very near the main railway station.

Getting tickets

Coaches work with the same system as buses and trams (see above).

Metropolitana (underground/subway)

Obviously only the largest cities (Rome, Milan, Naples) have a *Metropolitana*. None has more than two lines, so they are nowhere near as extensive as the buses. However, they are cheap and fairly reliable, so it is usually worth using them whenever you can in order to avoid the traffic hold-ups which are so common above ground.

Getting tickets

At the moment metro tickets cost 1 000 lire, and they allow you to go anywhere on the network. Most stations have ticket machines only, so unless you have a season ticket you will need to keep loose change on you. They do not take paper money.

Air

Because Italy is long and narrow, internal flights are quite common, especially among business people. Not surprisingly, they are much more expensive than the train. Unless you find an exceptionally well paid job, it is unlikely that you will be able to afford to fly around, although you may be tempted after a few 10-hour train journeys. At time of writing, you can fly from Rome to Milan for just over 300 000 lire – about the same as a flight to London.

Taxis

They are bright yellow and can be found near railway stations. Every time you come out of a station with a bag in your hand you will be offered a taxi by the unauthorized operators. They are more expensive, so avoid them. However, the authorized ones are hardly cheap. There are all sorts of surcharges which tend to be piled on to the flat rate for night trips, double rate for holidays, and more for heavy luggage.

For some reason in Italy, it is not that simple to pick up the phone and call a cab. Instead of their coming to you, you usually have to find them and many are not available 24 hours.

Car

In almost all Italian cities traffic is a problem, so unless you intend going out of town a lot, a car is probably more trouble than it is worth. Quite apart from the slowness of getting about cities in cars, there are often circulation restrictions as authorities attempt to do something drastic about pollution. Other drawbacks are the high price of petrol, the *pedaggi* (toll stations) on all *autostrade* and the fact that most cars are broken into or stolen at least once or twice in their lifetime. While Italian drivers often appear wild and undisciplined, they are actually very skilful and manage to avoid crashing most of the time. Respect for road laws is usually restricted to times when the *Vigili Urbani* or *Polizia Stradale* (both types of traffic police) are in evidence and so for foreign drivers the first time out on the streets of Rome or Naples can be quite hair-raising.

If, after all this, you still want to get a car you can get some second-hand bargains through local newspapers. Naturally bureaucratic hassles are in abundance. You must:

- be a resident;
- pay *passaggio di proprietà* (ownership transfer), until recently about 200 000 lire;
- wait two years for your *libretto di circolazione* (log book) to arrive;
- in the meantime either get a *foglio sostitutivo* (provisional document), which has to be renewed every three months, or hope you don't get stopped;
- change your driving licence to an Italian one (see below).

You must also be insured to drive, and unfortunately this is more expensive than in other countries, although it can be done relatively quickly at any *assicuratore* (insurer's).

Changing your driving licence

To do this you must take the following documents to your local *Prefettura*, the address of which you will find in the phone-book (the phrase *in bollo* means that the document has to be on *carta bollata* (special stamped paper) which you can get from most tobacconists):

- Typed application to the *Prefettura* – *in bollo* 15 000 lire.
- Residency certificate – *in bollo* 15 000 lire.
- 3 photos, one of which is authenticated – *in bollo* 15 000 lire.
- Special *marca da bollo* stamps – 15 000 lire.
- Receipts of the following payments into Post Office accounts: (a) 50 000 lire to account No 8003; (b) 15 000 lire to account

No 4028; (c) 10 000 lire to account No 9001.
- An authenticated photocopy of your driving licence – *in bollo* 15 000 lire.
- Medical certificate with photo.

Moped/Vespa

If you live in a city this is the only way to move about quickly. This simple truth is now so central to urban life that not just teenagers and students have them, but many business people use them too. In fact, in the busiest parts of most cities there are more people on two wheels than on four.

Theoretically mopeds (*motorini* in Italian) have to obey the same traffic rules as all other road users, but in practice you can go pretty much where you like and the traffic police will rarely bother to stop you.

Buying one second-hand is quite simple, and for 500 000 lire you should get something serviceable. Most local newspapers have a section devoted to buying and selling motor vehicles. Apart from an annual tax of 7 500 lire (up to 50 cc) there is very little paperwork or tax involved in having a *motorino*.

Foot

There is only one thing to be said about going places on foot and that is that you have far fewer rights as a pedestrian than you might imagine. Even at zebra-crossings motorists will not stop for you to cross unless you are right in front of their bumper, and even then with very bad grace. If you are knocked down by a car it is up to you, rather than the driver, to prove that it was not your fault. Be prepared, and when crossing be decisive – otherwise you will be stepping on and off the pavement for hours.

PERSONAL SECURITY AND THE POLICE

Despite Italy's fame for organized crime in the form of Mafia or corrupt politicians, most foreigners never come across anything more serious than petty theft. You are most at risk when travelling and, as all the guidebooks tell you, the places where you need to be especially careful are around train stations, on public transport, and anywhere where there are crowds.

Major cities (Rome and Naples especially) are very bad in summer, when the hordes of tourists arrive. Gangs of *scippatori* (bag-snatchers) wait around for likely-looking victims, which basically means foreigners, and when they see a chance they pounce with frightening speed, grabbing handbags, cameras, jewellery, and anything that looks valuable. They often work on mopeds, so by the time you have realized what is happening they are already far away.

Less dramatic, but equally distressing, are the pickpockets, who work in train stations, buses and any crowded place. Beware too of bands of gypsy children waving pieces of card – they are out to fleece you.

Much of the above is avoidable as long as you take the obvious precautions:

- Don't carry your wallet in your back pocket.
- Don't flash money or valuables about in public.
- Keep a firm hand on bags and cameras.
- Never leave valuables in a car.

I was once walking down one of the busy passages of the metro, on my way to pay the deposit on a flat, when I suddenly found myself surrounded by six or seven gypsy children. They started kissing their fingers and then patting my body, at the same time thrusting bits of cardboard up at me. Not knowing what was happening, I stopped and started reading what was written on the cards. A moment later they all ran away, leaving me bewildered but apparently none the worse for wear. It was only later that I discovered I no longer had my passport, my travellers' cheques or the 1 million lire I had just taken out of the bank. This is a standard trick. They watch for people withdrawing large amounts of money, accost them in the underground, patting your clothes to see where the money is, and distract you with the bits of card. Needless to say I never saw any of my property again.

Women and Italian men

Italian men have a very bad name in the rest of the world. This ill repute is only partly justified. It is true that harassment such as wolf-whistling, kerb-crawling and groping hands on the bus are more common in Italy than, for example, in the UK. However, the molestation is almost never violent – usually it is simply infuriating.

Foreign women sometimes find themselves in sticky situations for a number of reasons. First, they are not used to the amount of attention from men which is normal in Italy and so they have not developed ways of dealing with it. Second, young Italian males do in fact sometimes home in on foreign women. This is partly from fascination with the exotic, partly because of the myth of sexual freedom abroad, and partly because they think they can get away with it – foreign women, unaccompanied and away from the family, seem defenceless. Unfortunately, simply being alone seems to make you fair game, especially on beaches and in bars. It gets noticeably worse the further south you go. The only sure protection is to be in the company of a man.

If you find yourself being pestered, as long as it does not get physical, your best response is none at all. A look of indifference or boredom may achieve what no amount of words can. Talking is a bad move, because whatever you say you will be pulled into a dialogue which will be annoying and difficult to close.

If the situation gets overwhelming, shout '*Vaffanculo!*' ('Fuck off!') or '*Lasciatemi in pace!*' ('Leave me alone!'). A slap in the face is always an option too. Passivity to physical harassment will be read as permission to continue.

The police

In Italy there are four different police forces whose duties frequently overlap. The theory behind this peculiar state of affairs is that one united police force would have far too much power in its hands and would leave the way open for a *coup d'état*. As things stand, there is often fierce competition between the forces, hardly any cooperation, and often mutual dislike. One of the few things they have in common is a reputation for arrogance and incompetence. Thankfully this is less true now than it was, but you will no doubt come across incidents which leave you shocked/amazed/ indignant.

In contrast to the police in the rest of Europe, Italians have the smartest, most stylish upholders of law and order imaginable. When the *Carabinieri* decided to change their uniform in 1988, they called in Giorgio Armani. The four official police forces are:

- *I Carabinieri*. This all-male force is technically part of the military and is usually better trained and more reliable than *La Polizia*. If you have the choice, go to one of them for help. They do have a reputation for stupidity but this bears the same relation to the truth as do British jokes about the Irish. The uniform is dark blue with a wide red stripe down the trousers. They wear peaked caps and white leather cartridge belts.
- *La Polizia*. These are the ones who drive around very fast in light blue and white cars, waving big red lolly-pop sticks out of the window. For some reason they are rarely very polite or friendly. The uniform is: smoky-blue trousers with bright pink leg-stripe, navy blue jacket and navy-blue peaked cap. There are now several women in the force.
- *La Guardia di Finanza*. Their uniforms are light grey with green beret. Their job is to fight tax evasion and smuggling (especially

drugs) so they will not do anything if they see you parking illegally or going through a red light. On the other hand, they have been known to fine people for leaving a shop without a till-receipt.

- *I Vigili Urbani.* Also called *Polizia Municipale* and *Polizia Metropolitana.* Unlike the others, they do not usually carry guns – they are not expected to confront major crime, just traffic offences and petty law-breakers on the streets. They wear navy-blue trousers, a white jacket and a white hat shaped like an English policeman's. They have a reputation for being slack and for their ongoing feud with *La Polizia.*

When dealing with the police, remember that they do not consider themselves public servants, with a duty to you, the public. Any lack of respect on your part will work against you. Another thing to be aware of is that small crimes like bag-snatching or mugging are considered too minor to report. The chances of catching the culprit are so remote that Italians never bother. If you are insured, however, it is worth making a *denuncia* (official statement) at the *Questura* (police station), because the police report will be necessary for any claim you make.

Note that there are lots of other private security forces to be seen driving round the streets of any city. They may look like police but they are not, and they are liable to be anything but friendly.

Emergencies

In case of emergency take a note of the following nationwide telephone numbers:

112 for the police (*Carabinieri*).
113 for any emergency service.
115 for the Fire Brigade (*Vigili del Fuoco*).
116 for road assistance.

ENTERTAINMENT AND TIME OUT

Drinking

Drinking alcohol is not the social pastime that it is in Northern Europe and Italians, even when they go out, consume relatively little. They can quite happily make one drink last all evening, though it must be said that this is also to do with the outrageous prices charged for drinks in night-spots. Quite apart from this, being drunk is socially quite unacceptable and many people will tell you, quite honestly, that they have never had the experience. For women especially it is seen as nigh on a disgrace.

One of the reasons for this, bemoaned by many an English-speaker, is that Italians do not need alcohol to relax and have a good time. They drink wine or perhaps beer with a meal but this is because it is part of the meal, not for any social reasons. In general everything that you could want to drink is available; bars are always well stocked with spirits of all kinds. It is just that Italians prefer to go out for a coffee or an ice-cream after dinner, when many people in the UK, for example, would be off looking for the pub.

If you want to go out 'for a drink' these are your options:

Bar. This is a very vague term. In bars you can get virtually any kind of drink you want, from tea and coffee right through to beer, spirits and aperitifs. Often though they are not particularly conducive to a relaxed sit-down with a beer and friends. There is frequently nowhere to sit and when there is you usually have to pay more for the privilege of using it. Bars really cater for the Italian habit of taking a break from work or shopping and having a quick coffee or fruit-juice. Customers are usually in and out within five minutes. What is more, most bars close in the early evening. The ones that do not, stay open either to sell cigarettes or because they have pretensions to be a *locale* (see below).

Birreria. These are the nearest you will get to a British 'pub', and as the name suggests they concentrate on *birra* (beer). They usually have the same range of spirits and other drinks as a bar and probably offer some sort of food too. Often *birrerie* try to make the interior decor homely, and you can sit down at a table and be quite comfortable. Sometimes they call themselves pubs (pronounced 'pab') and the British will probably find themselves most at home here. They are frequented mainly by young people who do not want the hassle of dressing up for a *locale*. However, Italians being what they are, people generally do want to dress up and consequently *locali* are more popular.

Locali. *Locale* means something like 'night-spot', so the term is also used for nightclubs. However, trendy night-time bars like to call themselves *locali* too because it has a glamourous ring to it. These places generally make an effort to look hip and chic and they are correspondingly expensive. They often have live music and people dress up to go there. It is where a large portion of Italian night-life takes place, but the emphasis is less on drinking than seeing and being seen. They are usually waiter/waitress service and you frequently have to pay to get in. Some are for members only, but if you have the cash it is not a problem to become one. Confusingly, their names often involve 'bar' but they are easy to distinguish from the more everyday variety by the type of clientele they attract and the fact that they do not open till about 9 pm.

Cinema

Thanks to its high-flying cinematographic history Italy has a large and discerning film-going public. The facilities in all the cities are excellent and despite the fact that there are no multi-screens, the large number of cinemas means that you are unlikely to miss any film you would have seen back home. The one drawback is that almost all films are dubbed into Italian. There seems to be a growing tendency however to show films in their *lingua originale* every now and then, so at least in the cities it should be possible to see a few films in English. The following is a list of cinemas which show undubbed films some, if not all, of the time:

> *Bologna*: **Adriano**, Via San Felice 52 (tel: 051 555127); **Tiffany d'Essai**, Piazza di Porta Saragozza (tel: 051 585253).
> *Florence*: **Astro Cinema**, Piazza San Simone; **Cinema Atelier e Fiamma** (tel: 055 587307).
> *Genoa*: **Cineclub Cappuccini**, Via Cappuccini 1 (tel: 010 880069); **Cineclub Lumiere**, Via Vitale (tel: 010 50593).
> *Milan*: **Anteo**, Via Milazzo 9 (tel: 02 6597732); **Arcobaleno**, Viale Tunisia 11 (tel: 02 29406054); **Mexico**, Via Savone 57 (tel: 02 48951802).
> *Rome*: **Pasquino**, Vicolo del Piede 19 (tel: 06 5803622).
> *Turin*: **Cinema Cuore**, Via Nizza 56 (tel: 011 5617144); **Stand In Cinema**, Via dei Quartieri (tel: 011 4366771).

Apart from the above, the British Council establishments in Milan, Naples and Rome also have fairly frequent showings of British films.

Most newspapers carry a listings page, with their own credit ratings. Generally there are screenings at 16.30, 18.30, 20.30 and 22.30. Weekends tend to be very busy, so it is advisable to get there at least half an hour early to be sure of a seat. At time of writing the price of a seat is about 10 000 lire but there are sometimes discounts during the week, and if you go regularly some cities offer film-club cards which give you concessions at less popular times.

Italian cinemas always have an interval halfway through the film when you can get your ice-creams, pop-corn, or go out for a quick smoke.

Theatre

Despite having given the world *Commedia dell'Arte* and Luigi Pirandello, contemporary Italian theatre could hardly be said to be thriving. Dario Fo and the Neapolitan Eduardo De Filippo are the only two names which spring to mind, and outside Italy their fame is limited.

Part of the problem is that there are very few drama schools in Italy, so there has been little opportunity for a contemporary scene to develop. This leaves theatre-goers (in big cities) with a choice of conservative performances of international classics at the important venues and poorly funded, almost amateur dramatics elsewhere.

Most daily newspapers give full theatre listings on one of the final pages.

TV and radio

There are literally hundreds of TV stations operating in Italy, but only about ten are nationwide. RAI (Radio Televisione Italiana) owns three, Silvio Berlusconi's Fininvest corporation owns three more and the others are independent too. All channels (especially the privates) pump out huge quantities of advertising, and watching films can be very trying, as every fifteen minutes brings a commercial break.

RAI-UNO. The first of the state channels, this was for a long time held to be the mouthpiece of the Democrazia Cristiana. It is probably Italy's most popular channel, offering straight family viewing. Similar in many ways to the UK's BBC1.

RAI-DUE. The second state channel, offering more of the above but the news (*Telegiornale*) was from a more Socialist standpoint, until they ceased to be a political force.

RAI-TRE. Number three from the RAI was until recently the Communist slice of national TV. It still retains a slightly non-establishment stance, catering for more minority interests and sometimes has more original programmes. Considered by many to be the best of Italian TV.

CANALE 5. One of Berlusconi's stations, very commercial in outlook, modelled on the US network format. Lots of game/quiz shows.

ITALIA 1. Another of Berlusconi's, more of the above with lots of 'Telefilms' – Starsky and Hutch, the A-Team, etc, but no news.

RETE 4. Berlusconi again, similar to *Canale 5* with some awful soap operas.

ITALIA 7. Moving down-market, renowned for little apart from *Colpo Grosso*, a peculiar programme which claims to be a quiz show and involves a lot of women dancing with no clothes on.

TELEMONTECARLO. Films, soaps and reasonable news service. It hooks into CNN at about 2 am every day so you can hear some news in English if you are not asleep.

VIDEOMUSIC. As the name suggests, 24-hour music videos along the lines of MTV.

RETE A. Features stultifying advertising programmes interspersed with the odd soap (*Telenovela*).

Radio. In Italy, radio, like TV, offers hundreds of stations. The RAI runs five: Radio 1 and Radio 2 (a light selection of music, comedy and chat-shows), Radio 3 (classical music, discussions); and Radio 1-Rock and Radio 2-Rock (non-stop pop music, not only Italian). The BBC World Service is almost impossible to pick up in most parts of Italy unless you have a special shortwave radio.

Music

The Italian rock and pop scene is divided between fairly big acts from the UK and the USA and the homegrown singer/songwriter genre. The youth of today seems to go for mainstream English-speaking bands, and, as in most places, there are the same distinct factions: teenagers into heavy metal; student-types into dark, angst-ridden rock; smarter disco-goers who like anything modern and danceable (techno, house and all its offshoots); and the majority who simply go with the flow.

Slightly older 'young' people seem to prefer Italian solo singers, who for some reason vastly outnumber bands. Many of them have been around for a long time and an unkind view would be that the nation has not been able to find anything to replace them.

Many foreigners are highly critical of the Italian music scene, saying that it is mediocre and lacking in originality. The annual Festival of San Remo, the highlight of the pop music year, is largely ignored by the rest of the world, and indeed for anyone used to the Anglo-Saxon view of rock and roll there is little to recommend it.

On the other hand, it is worth remembering that the rest of the world still has not really accepted pop music in any other language than English. What is more, Italy has a completely different tradition of popular music which contrasts sharply with the metropolitan scenes of New York or London. Give it a chance before dismissing it entirely – Pino Daniele, Zucchero and others are at least as good as what is usually in your own country's charts.

Concerts

Most big names come to Italy in the course of touring, although some limit themselves to Milan and Rome. South of Rome, it has to be said, big concerts by foreign names are relatively few. For comprehensive listings pick up a copy of *Velvet*, the weekly music magazine, or simply keep an eye out for posters – most cities get plastered with them before any major concert. Tickets can usually be bought from record shops, or on the night itself from touts outside the venue.

On a more day-to-day level, if you want some live music Italy abounds in jazz clubs and piano bars. The former are generally worth visiting, the latter very rarely.

South American and Caribbean music is also in vogue at present, and if you are in a city that may be where the best action is. Details will be in most daily papers.

Nightlife

There is no shortage of nightclubs and discothèques in Italy; what is missing is any great difference between them. It is very rare to find venues that concentrate on one type of music, or that have a particular dress code. Both music and dress tend to conform unquestioningly to a fairly rigid model. The music is modern but always mainstream, sticking to well known Europop and dance music. The dress code is always clean-cut, well groomed and flash.

In Rome or Milan you might find a couple of places which very self-consciously propose an 'alternative' scene of sorts, but they are still squeaky clean compared to the dives which English-speaking youth likes to frequent. For a full list of the clubs and discothèques in your town consult the newspapers *Repubblica* or *Corriere della Sera* which usually have a page or two detailing the club scene (there is a different version published for each major city), and there you will find names, addresses and sometimes an indication of the type of music.

Admission prices start at about 15 000 lire but can be much more. For this you sometimes get a *prima consumazione* – ie your first drink free. Afterwards drinks are prohibitively expensive so buying rounds is not expected. Women can often get into discos free, especially if they have just opened, because owners know that the more women go the more popular the place will be. This is not to say, however, that they are good places for men to meet women. People usually go in large groups which tend to stick together. Going alone is generally a fairly unpleasant experience; for a woman it is considered 'cheap' and for a man simply pitiable.

In the summer many beach resorts have a selection of open-air discothèques which are certainly more comfortable than any indoor ones which remain open. They are very popular with young Italians, and it is here that you will find most nightlife during the summer months, not in the cities.

Here are recommendations for places to go in three major cities:

Milan:
Bar Magenta, Via Carducci 13. Trendy bar.
Hollywood, Corsi Como 15. Trendy club.
Pois, Via Piopette 1a. Bar/café.
Racana Pub, Via Sannio 18, British-style pub with a lot of British people.
Plastic, Viale Umbria 120. Gothic/punk club.
Nuova Idea, Via de Castiesa 30. Big gay disco.

Rome:
Alien, Via Velletri 13. Very hip disco.
Blackout, Via Saturnia 18. Disco, indie night Friday.
Soul II Soul, Via dei Fienaroli 30b. Soul/dance club.
L'Alibi, Via Monte Testaccio 44. Gay club.
Druids' Den, Via San Martino ai Monti 28. Irish pub.
Fiddler's Elbow, Via dell'Omarta. Another Irish pub.
La Vetrina, Via della Vetrina 20. Lively, trendy bar.

Naples:
Murat, Via Bellini. Live music.
Gauguin, Via Bellini. Live music.
Notting Hill, Piazza Dante. Reggae/rap venue.
Vineria del Centro, Via Paladino. Trendy pub.
Frame Café, Via Paladino. As above.
Riot, Via San Biaggio dei Librai. Alternative hang-out.
Chez Moi, Parco Margherita 13. Straightforward disco.
KGB (currently changing venue). Rock/indie club.

Sport

Sport has not always been as important in Italy as it is now. At schools children are rarely given the time or opportunity to practise sports. There is also a serious lack of municipal sports facilities, meaning that taking up any sport is usually a fairly costly business.

Had it not become fashionable in the 1980s to spend time and money on fitness and health, sport would probably still be ignored by most Italians. Thanks to some cunning marketing by sportswear designers, sport is now seen as another chance to dress up, look good, and make a *bella figura*. Quite apart from this, Italy's climate makes it perfect for all outdoor sports.

Finding out where public sports facilities are is not easy. Try looking in the *Pagine Gialle* (Yellow Pages) under the name of the sport you want, or under 'Sport' in general. Nearly all sports have the same name as in English, or very similar – *il tennis*; *lo squash*; *il rugby*; etc. The only exception is soccer which is called *calcio*. Swimming pools are *piscina* and are not as numerous as in other countries.

Basketball. Known as either *Basket* or *Pallacanestra*, this is probably Italy's favourite sport after soccer. There will definitely be a club near you, but you will have to be pretty good to gain admittance.

Cycling. Cycling is very popular both as a spectator sport and as something to do yourself on an amateur level. Naturally the geography of some regions makes them better suited than others, so it has a higher profile in Emilia-Romagna for example than in the mountainous areas of Basilicata. With the arrival of 'mountain bikes' and trendy cycling clothing, it's quite the thing to do (and to be seen doing).

Soccer. Both as a spectator sport and for active participation, soccer is Italy's national sport. Ever since winning the World Cup in 1982 Italians have called their league *il campionato più bello del mondo* (the world's most beautiful/greatest).

While this is debatable, it is true that very few other countries devote as much time, money and media attention to the sport. This is largely due to the huge expectations which Italian soccer has created for itself, expectations which it tries to satisfy by regularly importing international stars, luring them with astronomical salaries.

Going to see a match in Italy is undeniably a thrilling experience and vary rarely involves any of the violence for which British football is known. Italian fans (*tifosi*) get excited but without alcohol, and they generally stay good-natured.

The best place to get tickets for a match is from the ground itself, a good while in advance if the match is an important one. If you arrive without a ticket, very often you will be able to get one from a tout, but you can end up paying a lot more than the original price. Sunday league matches cost around 25 000 lire for the cheapest tickets.

Golf. Completely ignored in Italy for a long time, golf is gaining some ground. A few courses have been built and it is starting to be taken up by well-off business men. The scarcity of facilities and the type of customer they are aimed at means, however, that golf is an expensive hobby in Italy.

Palestra. This means a gym or fitness centre where you go to work out. Although not really a sport, it is worthy of mention because of the numbers of Italians who make it a big part of their lives. There are now *palestre* on every street corner, and for a modest membership fee you can use all the equipment and have some one tell you what to do to build up or slim down this or that part of your body.

Rugby (Union). Rugby has only recently come to the country's attention, but is quickly gaining currency. The Italian national team performed very respectably at the last Rugby World Cup and is second only to France in Continental Europe.

Skiing. Most of the young population heads north at some point during the winter for the ritual *settimana bianca"* (a week of skiing). Most of the ski resorts are in the northern regions of Piemonte, Val d'Aosta and Trentino-Alto Adige where the Alps and the Dolomites offer skiing as good as anywhere in Europe.

Tennis. As the sport steadily grows more and more popular, there are now pretty good facilities in most towns and even in some remoter places too. *Campi* (courts) are usually clay – grass courts are almost unheard of. Courts are usually busy in the summer months so ring a few days in advance to be sure of playing when you want to.

Volleyball. Known simply as *volley*, volleyball is immensely popular among young people because you can play almost anywhere, with any number of people. It is a very common beach activity. There is also an amateur league which is developing a committed band of spectator followers.

Going to the beach

During the summer this is a big part of many Italians' free time. If you live anywhere near the sea you will probably be invited sooner or later to accompany a group of people *al mare*. If you accept, go prepared. Italians take the whole business very seriously. This means dressing well on the beach, working hard on getting a perfectly even tan, and probably indulging in some sort of ball-game on just that bit of sand where you want to walk.

Thanks to the persistent demand, transport to and from the beach is generally well organized. In very popular areas traffic can be horrendous in the morning as people arrive and in the evening as they go home. The train is probably the least stressful way of getting to a beach – that is unless you live right on the coast. In this case, a moped is ideal for dodging traffic and finding the best beaches.

Beaches in Italy are either *spiaggia libera* (free beach) or *stabilimenti* (privately owned sections of beach which you have to pay to visit). In the case of the former, there may well be a bar on the beach if it is popular, but other facilities like toilets and showers will probably be missing. In the *stabilimenti*, on the other hand, you will have everything you could possibly desire while on the beach, from sun-beds and umbrellas to restaurants and swimming pool. Entry prices vary, but are usually about 4 000 lire. Anything else you want costs more of course.

Going topless is very much accepted practice on Italian beaches although it might attract unwanted attention the further south you go, especially if women are unaccompanied by men.

FOOD, DRINK AND EATING OUT

Italians have a passionate relationship with their food and are notoriously bad at accepting the cuisine of other countries, even when on holiday there. In fact 'Italian cuisine' is really a collection of regional cuisines, and for this reason it is rich and varied. Let's start by looking at what they eat and drink.

Food

The traditional Mediterranean diet based on fish, olive oil and pasta, with lots of fresh fruit and vegetables, is widely accepted as one of the healthiest in the world. In fact it is gradually being eroded by faster convenience foods as women leave kitchens and start working, and so have less time for cooking.

Nevertheless, Italian classics like pasta and pizza (both of which originated in Naples) continue to dominate, although pizza is rarely made at home now. In the north *polenta* (a savoury dish a bit like semolina) used to be a common alternative to pasta. It is still eaten but pasta has become the staple there too.

Since the second world war, meat has become far more widely eaten and as a result today's younger generation is considerably taller and more robust than its predecessor.

The three main meals are:

- *Colazione* (breakfast): usually coffee with biscuits or *cornetti* (jam- or custard-filled croissants).
- *Pranzo* (lunch): traditionally this was quite a substantial meal with mounds of pasta, meat, vegetables and fruit but, as more and more people work in offices and have to get back to work, faster and lighter substitutes are more popular.
- *Cena* (dinner): definitely the main meal of the day. It is usually eaten quite late, 8 or 8.30 pm at the earliest, and involves more pasta, meat and vegetables. Generally, if you have had pasta at lunch you do not have it at dinner, and *vice versa*, although this is by no means a hard-and-fast rule.

Pasta

Finally, a word or two about pasta.

It can have virtually anything on it, the simplest form being with garlic and oil, but at the other extreme it can be weighed down with meat, fish and vegetables of all sorts.

It can be *in bianco* (white) or *rosso* (red), which means with or without tomato sauce.

For most Italians, it should be *al dente* (literally, 'to the tooth'), which means it should still offer a minimal resistance to being cut or bitten. Foreigners do not have a hope of getting it right and are usually accused of creating a flaccid, textureless mess.

You do not put Parmesan cheese on all pasta dishes, but the rules are so complex that your only hope is to watch what other people do.

The numerous shapes pasta can take correspond to the sort of sauces and condiments that you eat with them. The situation is further complicated by individual preferences for the various types. While most foreigners think that pasta is pasta is pasta, people who have stayed here long enough to know claim that there is in fact a noticeable difference between a dish of quills and a dish of twists with the same sauce. Presumably it has something to do with the way the sauce adheres to individual pieces of pasta.

When eating spaghetti you should turn your fork clockwise, and it is considered rude to leave strands hanging out of your mouth which you then suck up. However Italians love to see the mess foreigners make when eating it, so your initial clumsiness will be more a cause of amusement than of offence.

Drink

With a few minor exceptions Italians drink the same things as people in the English-speaking world. Their habits are sometimes different and where this is the case I have included details, so you can avoid making a *brutta figura*.

Aperativi. Aperitifs like Martini are drunk very quickly and only as a preliminary to a meal. Italians do not like drinking alcohol away from the dinner table, and no amount of flash advertising seems to be able to change this.

Coffee. In Italy coffee comes in an astonishing array of variations. They are: *caffè espresso*, the most common variety – a very small quantity of very strong coffee in a very small cup; *caffè lungo* – the same but with a little more water and therefore marginally more *lungo*; *caffè corretto* – normal espresso with a drop of *grappa*, whisky or something similar; *caffè macchiato* – the same basic coffee with a splash of milk (*macchiato* means 'stained'); *latte macchiato* – the reverse of the above, ie a glass of hot milk with a splash of coffee; *cappuccino* – the one everybody has heard of – coffee fluffed up with hot milk. (Beware! Italians love to see foreigners taking *cappuccino* at all times of the day, oblivious to the fact that it is considered a breakfast or at least a morning drink.)

Digestivi. Like *aperativi*, digestives exist as part of the meal and not as an independent drinking option. The classic end to a meal in an Italian restaurant is a round of *grappa* (a white spirit made from grapes) or *amaro* (a black spirit made from aromatic herbs with a bitter taste).

Mineral water. Growing concern for health and fitness has made mineral waters very fashionable in recent years and it is unusual to find a household fridge or a restaurant table without a bottle. The perennial battle between *gasata* (fizzy) and *naturale* (still) rages on with the latter starting to take the upper hand.

On one of my first evenings out in Italy, I ate in a restaurant with some colleagues from work and then we went to a cosy little bar for coffee. We sat down and I waited eagerly for a nice mug of coffee to arrive. What duly arrived was a tiny glass containing perhaps a centimetre of dark brown viscous fluid. When my friends had persuaded me that this was my coffee, I tried it and found that it was in fact coffee, albeit much shorter and stronger than I had expected.

Ian Cambell (Australia)

Tea. If you are a tea-lover it may be hard to find satisfaction in Italy unless you make your own. In a bar you will be served a cup of hot water with a teabag in the saucer and, unless you say you want milk, they will probably automatically give you a slice of lemon. Most Italians consider tea with milk quite disgusting. Tea in general is not held in great esteem, and even when an Italian deigns to touch the stuff it is with so much sugar and lemon that the fact that it is tea is quite unnoticeable. There is an irritatingly common myth in Italy that the English (and by extension, English speakers) always have a ceremony called 'Tea' at 5 pm. It will be referred to time and time again, in fact every time you are seen in the company of the stuff.

Wine. Very little of the wine sold in your local *enoteca* is anything other than Italian or possibly French. Justifiably, Italians are quite satisfied with their own wines and often do not know anything about wines from other countries. Thankfully this means that wine snobs are few and far between.

Italians drink 90 litres of wine per head each year and almost all of this is drunk with meals. It is very rarely drunk in bars, and the concept of 'wine bars' is quite alien as wine is so closely bound up with eating.

Some of the best wine you will drink will be local homemade stuff that has no label and is unavailable in shops. You might come across it if you are invited to somebody's house and the best compliment you can pay to a your host is to drink his wine, and visibly appreciate it.

When buying wines from the shops, the letters DOCG (*Denominazione di Origine Controllata Garantita*) guarantee a certain quality, although many good wines are not yet covered by the DOC system. In restaurants, however, most people are quite satisfied with the table wine (*vino da tavola*).

Eating out

If you are used to the cosmopolitan eating habits of New York or London you may be disappointed, as foreign food has never really taken a hold in Italy. Italians tend to stick to what they know when it comes to eating out, so, apart from the odd Chinese restaurant, you are basically limited to eating Italian. Nevertheless, Italian cuisine is in itself quite varied thanks to the numerous regional influences it draws on, and so few people have serious cause for complaint.

There is also a wide range of eating places, with something to suit everyone's pocket. In general terms the possibilities are as follows, in ascending order of cost.

Bars. Bars are mostly open all day and they nearly all offer a range of snacks for between 2 000 and 3 000 lire. The choice is usually limited to *tramezzini* (sandwiches), *pizzette* (little pizzas), or *medaglioni* (toasted sandwiches), although increasingly bars are trying to cash in on the demand for cheap lunchtime eating by offering salads, simple pasta dishes and hamburger-like fast food. As long as you do not expect anything too lavish, bars can provide quite satisfactory daytime eating.

> To start to feel at home in any Italian city or town, I think that the best thing you can do is to adopt a *Bar-Pasticceria*. Find one that's near your home, preferably one that looks clean and in which the people seem friendly, and go there every morning for a cappuccino and a pastry. First of all Italians appreciate foreigners that drink cappuccino at the right time (before 10.30 am), and secondly you can't help feeling part of things, because you're doing the same thing as millions of Italians all over the country. Sooner or later people start nodding at you, and before you know it you're exchanging daily trivia and talking about football as if you'd done it all your life.
>
> *Dave Cooke (UK)*

Fast food. Now all Italian cities have the usual selection of fast-food joints catering to a young market which eats quickly and makes few demands. As these places are the same the world over, there is little point describing them at any length. A cheeseburger with French fries will currently cost you about 7 000 lire.

Rosticcerie/tavola calda. These offer slightly more Italian fast food and cost a little more than the above. Standard fare is roast chicken; fried potatoes; various vegetables; lasagne; spaghetti alla bolognese; and a couple of other types of pasta. These are all displayed on a glass-fronted hot plate and you choose what you want. You can generally eat in or take away – if you decide to eat in, the surroundings are rarely conducive to having a peaceful meal. To get a reasonable meal you will have to spend about 10 000 lire.

Pizzeria. They can vary enormously in terms of service, quality and decor, but as a rule of thumb try to avoid places which are obviously frequented by tourists – the prices will be inflated and the quality poor. Because they are so popular, service tends to be brisk and waiters will often expect you to know what you want almost before you sit down. For Italians this is quite reasonable seeing that *pizzerias* offer more or less the same things wherever you go. You are quite at liberty to order a pizza and leave it at that, but you will probably be offered *bruschetta* (toast with fresh tomatoes or some other topping) as a starter and possibly *suppli* (rice croquettes) as well. Keeping things at a minimum you would be hard pushed to spend less than 12 000 or 13 000 lire per head. (For different types of pizza, see Appendix 5.)

Trattoria/ristorante. There is technically a difference between the two types of establishment, but very often places call themselves both so the distinction is all but lost. In theory *trattorie* are more traditional in terms of food, but whatever the difference the prices are much the same. In English they would both be 'restaurants' and they (usually) offer exactly what you would expect from those – good quality food, served in pleasant surroundings for prices from middle-of-the-range to expensive.

Italian restaurants have between 3 and 5 courses: *anti-pasto* (hors d'oeuvres); *primo* (usually pasta); *secondo* (meat or fish); *contorno* (salad or vegetables); *dolce/frutta* (dessert or fruit). You can safely skip any of these, although 2 courses is considered an absolute minimum. You should expect to spend upwards of 25 000 lire for three courses. Of course it also depends on how much you drink.

Paying and tipping

In restaurants and pizzerias you pay by asking for *il conto* and then either leaving the money on the table or, if you want change, taking it to the cash till. Strictly speaking you should not leave the place until you have been given a *ricevuta fiscale* (a bill with the owner's tax details on it) because if you do they can avoid paying tax on what you spend. Usually they do give you one, but if they do not you will have to decide whether or not you care about their tax evasion.

When eating out in groups, Italians usually divide the bill by the number of people, irrespective of what each person had. It is considered bad form to try to work out exactly what each individual owes.

Nowadays, most restaurants add a 10% service charge to the bill, so in theory tipping is not necessary unless you think you have had particularly good service. Nevertheless, Italians often round the bill up to the nearest 10 000 lire anyway.

SHOPPING

Shops (*negozi*) and businesses are generally open between 9 am and 1 pm, and then from about 4 pm till 7 or 8 pm. In the early afternoon you are unlikely to find anything open other than bars. On Sundays, everything is closed except for a few bars and *pasticcerie* (in the morning). Here is a list of shop names:

Bakery	*Paneficio* (usually sells only bread)
Bookshop	*Libreria* (remember 'library' is *biblioteca*)
Butcher's	*Macelleria*
Cake shop	*Pasticcerria* (a huge range of cakes and sweet things)
Chemist's	*Farmacia*
Greengrocer	*Fruttivendolo*
Grocer	*Alimentari* (a wide range of supplies, from foodstuffs to toilet paper to washing up liquid)
Hairdresser	*Parrucchiere*
Ironmonger	*Ferramenta* (for all sorts of hardware, including basic electrical equipment like plugs and cables)
Jeweller's	*Gioielleria*
Newsagent	*Edicola* (this is a newspaper kiosk; for some reason newspaper vendors never seem to have shops)
Stationer's	*Cartoleria* (often together with a *libreria*)
Supermarket	*Supermercato* (often not much different from a large *alimentari*)
Tobacconist	*Tabaccaio* (these shops always have a sign outside with a white 'T' on a black background)
Wine shop	*Enoteca* (you can find wine in most bars, *alimentari* and supermarkets as well, but the choice is better in an *enoteca*)

I used to get so angry when I was standing waiting to be served in shops and bars and people would come in, walk straight past me up to the counter and demand this, that or the other. Not only this, the height of impertinence to my mind, but then the person serving often actually listened to them and gave them what they wanted. It took me a long time to accept that in Italy, if you want something, you say so, and it doesn't matter if you are interrupting. Now I march into shops, shout *Buon Giorno* so that they know I'm there, and as soon as I see anybody looking in my direction I tell them what I want.

Phillippa Hayward (UK)

Other types of shop tend not to have specific names, and are just called *negozio di . . .* (eg *negozio di hifi, negozio di computer*, etc).

Department stores tend to keep the same opening times as normal shops. The most common chains are: *Rinascente* – classy and expensive; *Coin* – quality goods, less expensive but not cheap; *Standa* – reliable wares for reasonable prices; *Upim* – very like *Standa*. The last two often have supermarkets in the basement, and are good for simple household requirements.

Shopping for clothes (see Table 2 for sizes) is always an expensive business in Italy. Whatever it is you want, you will find that you can get it cheaper back home. However, if you want that genuine 'Made in Italy' feel, try the department stores first. The prices tend to be more affordable than private boutiques. Markets too can be a cheaper option, but they are not always much cheaper and the quality of clothes on sale is sometimes very poor.

Table 2. Equivalent sizes for clothes.

Women's shirts/dresses

UK	10	12	14	16	18
USA	8	10	12	14	16
Italy	40	42	44	46	48

Sweaters

UK	10	12	14	16
USA	8	10	12	14
Italy	46	48	50	52

Table 2 continued.

Women's shoes

UK	3	4	5	6	7	8
USA	4	5	6	7	8	9
Italy	36	37	38	39	40	41

Men's shoes

UK	4	5	6	7	8	9	10	11
USA	7	7.5	8	9	10	10.5	11	12
Italy	37	38	39	40	41	42	43	44

Men's shirts

UK/USA	14	14.5	15	15.5	16	16.5	17	17.5
Italy	36	37	38	39	40	41	42	43

Men's suits

UK/USA	36	38	40	42	44	46
Italy	46	48	50	52	54	56

SOCIALIZING

Greetings

In social situations it is usual to shake hands with people you meet in whatever circumstance, whether the person is a friend you have known for years and last saw yesterday or someone you are meeting for the first time. If you know somebody, you then say '*Come stai*' or '*Come va*' ('How are you?'), or '*Come sta*' if you are not on first-name terms. In any other situation '*Buon giorno/ Buona sera*' is the norm. Another greeting is '*Salve*', which, because it is neutral, is useful if you are not sure exactly how you stand with the person – a professional acquaintance, for example.

When you introduce yourself or are being introduced, the accepted formula is to say '*Piacere*' ('Pleased to meet you'), say your name and offer your hand.

One Italian habit which might strike outsiders as strange is saying '*Buon giorno*' and '*Buona sera*' on entering shops. Obviously in supermarkets and large, impersonal stores it is not expected but elsewhere it is. You can repeat the same on leaving too, to which the assistant/owner will respond '*Arrivederci*'.

Kissing

Kissing is also common between friends, and again not simply because you have not seen someone for a long time. It is probably most frequent between women, and between men and women, but there are plenty of men who do it to their male friends too. Two kisses, one on each cheek.

Opinions vary on when you start kissing people socially, because it is obviously a personal matter. Some people kiss the first time they meet, some leave it a bit longer, but it is generally agreed that some sort of 'feeling' has to develop before it becomes natural. To avoid embarrassment, leave it to others to take the initiative. Finally do not kiss on the lips: that is what Mafiosi do when they are about to bump you off.

How to address people

Italian, like many other languages, provides more than one form of address. 'You' in English can be *tu*, *voi* or *lei*. *Tu* is used for people whom you would call by their first name, *voi* is formal like *vous* in French but rarely used nowadays. People prefer to use *lei* (literally 'she') as a way of indicating respect or distance. It can be quite tricky when learning the language to call your interlocuter 'she' and conjugate all the verbs accordingly. However, this would never be used in a social situation, and people tend to make allowances for foreigners.

Social life and friendship

In Italy social life is about being with people. What people do together is far less important than the simple fact of being in each other's company. Predictably the thing which strikes most foreigners about Italian social life is that people never actually seem to do anything. Young people tend to congregate in a *piazza* or some such meeting point, and then they simply 'hang out', letting the evening develop by itself. Any concrete proposal is usually discussed at such length that in the end it all seems too much fuss, and the idea is given up.

Older people get together for a *cena* (dinner) at somebody's house, or maybe go out for a pizza or to see a film. Going out for a drink is never really considered as an option. Far more likely is the idea of going out for an ice-cream or just a walk. In all towns and villages there is a place where people congregate in early evening for the daily ritual, the *passeggiata*. This means something like a 'stroll', but it serves more of a social function than anything else. You dress up, then wander around meeting people, chatting, having a look at everyone else, and then you go home.

When my birthday came round and I mentioned it to a few Italian friends, I was pleased when they asked if I wanted to go out for a pizza with everyone. I said yes, and on the appointed night we went out and had a very pleasant evening. When the waiter bought the bill and put it on the table I noticed everyone was ignoring it. I had assumed that when it was someone's birthday either the friends paid for everything or at the very least everyone paid for themselves. In fact, the custom is for the birthday boy/girl to pay for everybody. When I looked at the bill and put my share on the table, my friends very kindly saved me embarrassment by quickly paying up. It was only some time later that I discovered the truth.

Helen Lewis (UK)

Parties do happen, but they are probably not like the ones you are used to. They are very often birthday parties in the family home, with fizzy drinks, cakes and parents on hand. They are usually far too self-conscious affairs for there to be any dancing or other forms of letting your hair down.

In all these situations it is in fact very easy to make 'friends'. This is another respect in which Italians like to compare themselves with the 'cold, unfriendly English' (other English speakers do not seem to have this label attached to them), but you should be aware that, while you might apparently get on like a house on fire one evening, that does not necessarily mean a lasting friendship has been forged. Italians tend to get on with everybody in a way Anglo-Saxons do not, so it is easy to get the impression that you are a bosom pal when in fact you are simply a social acquaintance.

What all this means in practical terms is that, although striking up social relations is very easy, making friends who will still be interested in you next year takes just as long as it would in any English-speaking country.

A few points to remember:

- If you are invited to *cena*, always take something. A bottle of wine is OK, but it is better to take a dessert – ice-cream, or cakes (*dolci*).
- Social appointments are very elastic – punctuality is rare, and standing people up is not considered all that bad by some.
- Always present people if they do not know each other. It is considered rude not to do so.
- Burping or farting, even among friends, are absolutely not on. They never see the funny side.
- Getting drunk is an almost unforgiveable disgrace.

- If you have got a car, you are expected to give people lifts at the end of an evening together.

Talking to Italians

When you are still learning Italian, socializing can be a bit nerve-wracking, but there is no real reason not to have your say. Italians are justifiably renowned for being great communicators and even with only a handful of words at your disposal you will be able to get your meaning across. They are generally patient, willing to try to understand and they greatly appreciate any effort you make to speak in Italian. The golden rule is: don't be afraid to try – *buttati* (jump in), as the expression goes. Throw caution to the wind and you will be surprised at how much fun you can have with your dreadful pronunciation and ungrammatical phrases.

Don't be surprised at how direct Italians can be in conversation. They will freely tell you what they like and do not like about your clothes, house and basically anything they clap eyes on. They will also tend to ask all sorts of questions, some of which you may consider a little indelicate. Try not to be offended; no offence is meant. The best way to respond is in kind.

While most English-speakers feel a deep-seated reluctance to speak when someone else is doing so, this is not so with Italians. In a group of young, or even old people, it is quite normal for conversation to consist of everybody talking simultaneously at the tops of their voices. Speaking from experience this can be quite disturbing, especially if it happens when you are in the middle of saying something. Again the secret is not to get offended, but simply to join in. Talking over people is not considered rude and often it is either that or shut up.

Broadly speaking, Italy is not a good place in which to be shy or socially reserved. For naturally diffident people, adapting to the dynamics of Italian social groups can be very difficult, especially when you do not have complete mastery of the language. But it is

By the time I came to the end of my first year in Italy, I had a fairly decent social life going. I could speak Italian reasonably well, but I thought I would never really be a hit socially because I just wasn't by nature as bright and full of beans as my Italian friends seemed to be. When I got home for the summer break, I started seeing my old friends again. After a few evenings together, people were telling me that I had become a brighter, more energetic conversationalist, and also that I asserted myself much more forcefully than before.

Ann Sansum (New Zealand)

important to remember that the social life of a group consists primarily in talking, and if you do not contribute, for whatever motive, you may be regarded as being aloof. On the other hand, anything you give of yourself is automatically received with interest and enthusiasm.

Girlfriends/boyfriends

Finding and keeping them is no easier, nor more difficult than it is in the UK or the USA, for example. Women may find it easier than men, given that Italian men rarely disguise their interest, but there is no guarantee that you will like what's on offer.

Men should prepare themselves for long and confusing courtship rituals that sometimes lead nowhere.

On the whole, the fact that you are foreign is not a disadvantage when forming intimate relationships. Blonde hair and blue eyes generally go down very well.

7 | Italy and the Italians

This chapter provides a brief background to the geography, history, politics and culture of the country. It should be useful both as an introduction to Italy and as background knowledge for classroom conversations.

GEOGRAPHY AND CLIMATE

Geography

Italy is a long boot-shape and its territory spans over a thousand kilometres from Lombardy, on the Swiss border, to Sicily, only a stone's-throw from Tunisia. It has mountains which run its length, from the Alps and the Dolomites in the North, to the Appenines which are its backbone.

It is at the same time a Mediterranean and a Central European country, with all the diversity of people and customs which that implies. There are 19 regions, each with a distinct character which has not been lost in the short time since unification in 1861.

In the north is Italy's economic power-base, in the industrial triangle of Milan, Turin and Genova (Genoa). It is the home of Fiat and Olivetti and its 'capital', Milan, is an important centre of European fashion. Many of its people feel closer cultural ties to France or Germany than they do to Rome, the centre of national government.

The south, sometimes called *il Mezzogiorno*, is largely agricultural, and economically one of the poorest areas of Europe. It is here that the standard image of Italy is truest. The people are dark-skinned, talkative and at times distinctly amoral. Its 'capital', Naples, gave the world pizza, syphilis and Sophia Loren and it can strike the first-time visitor as an incarnation of sweaty pandemonium.

The landscape in the south tends to be dry and rocky, very harsh when compared to the hills and plains of the centre, and the cool mountains and lakes in the north.

Climate

Italy's climate is one of its major attractions; in general it has warm, dry summers and mild winters. That said, however, there are a few things to bear in mind. First, annual rainfall in Italy is about the same as in the much-maligned UK. The difference is that, while in the UK it rains gently a lot of the time, in Italy (especially in the south) it rains heavily but not too often. Of course, this pattern varies according to the region – in parts of the north you can find drizzle to compare with the greyest parts of Northern Europe. Conversely, the winters in Potenza and Benevento (central south) are often bitterly cold and snowbound. On the whole inland areas in the north have the coldest time of it in winter. Coastal towns never get cold enough to complain of, and in places like Palermo or Naples temperatures approaching freezing are almost unknown.

The pleasantest times of year are spring and autumn, when temperatures are comfortable and you are unlucky to get rain. Summers can be stiflingly hot in cities and most people head for the sea or the mountains. See Table 3 for an overview of seasonal temperatures in the cities.

Table 3. Average temperatures in the cities (°C).

	January	April	July	October
Ancona	5.7	13.6	24.9	16.6
Bari	8.4	13.9	24.5	18.2
Bologna	2.5	13.8	26.0	15.2
Florence	5.6	13.3	25.0	15.8
Genova	8.4	14.5	24.6	18.1
Milan	1.9	13.2	24.8	13.7
Naples	8.7	14.3	24.8	18.1
Palermo	10.3	16.2	25.3	19.9
Rome	7.4	14.4	25.7	17.7
Trieste	5.3	12.9	24.0	15.6
Venice	3.8	12.6	23.6	15.1

HISTORY

Knowing where to start the history of Italy is a problem in itself. While the modern nation with its current borders came into existence only in 1871, 'Italic' peoples have inhabited the peninsula since about 2000 BC, and as far back as the Paleolithic era

(1 000 000–70 000 BC) human settlements are known to have existed.

In the interests of creating a comprehensible and useful overview, I have divided this section into 7 parts, starting with the first Greeks and Etruscans and finishing with the end of the second world war.

Greeks and Etruscans

In the eighth century BC, Greek settlers founded colonies in Sicily and southern Italy which came to be known as Magna Grecia. At the same time, in the north of the peninsula the Etruscans were establishing themselves as the dominant tribe. They pushed out the indigenous Latins, Sabines and Ligurians, but traded more or less peacefully with the Greek colonies to the south. As the fledgling Roman state started to make its presence felt, the Etruscans avoided a major conflict and over time the two peoples merged.

Rome and the rise of the Empire

According to the legend it was two Etruscans, the brothers Romulus and Remus, who founded the city in 753 BC. Romulus, who almost immediately killed his brother, began a line of kings which continued while Rome flourished for over 150 years. The last Etruscan king was Tarquinius Superbus, who was kicked out in 509 BC to make way for the Roman Republic. The Republic then started conquering everywhere within reach – Italy, North Africa and other Mediterranean states.

After three centuries of growth, the expanding Empire inevitably came into conflict with Carthage (present-day Tunisia) and it took the three Punic Wars (260–146 BC) to establish Rome as the supreme military force in the Mediterranean. It was during the second of these wars that Hannibal's famous escapade with the elephants took place, in which he routed the the Roman army and laid waste to the capital.

Time went on, riches from all over the Empire flowed in, and the governing Roman class started to show signs of corruption. The underclasses revolted and in the Social War (91–87 BC) they fought for and attained the rights of Roman citizenship.

In 49 BC Julius Caesar came to the head of the empire and, as Shakespeare's play illustrates, was seen off by Brutus and company for getting too big for his boots. The subsequent battle for power was eventually won by Octavian (Caesar's nephew) whose main rival, Antony, was at the time somewhat distracted by the charms of Cleopatra (again, see Shakespeare).

So Octavian came to power and called himself Augustus Caesar. His reign (27 BC–14 AD) began 200 years of peace, which became known as the Pax Romana. During this time the Latin language was developed and diffused, and art flourished.

The fall of the Empire

The Empire continued to enjoy relative stability until the third century AD. The beginning of the end came when Goths, Franks and Alamanni started attacking the Empire, revealing how difficult to defend it had become. Diocletian (284–305), in an attempt to render the territory less cumbersome and more controllable, then divided it in two: an Eastern half centred on Constantinople and the Western half with himself as Emperor and his capital in Milan. Diocletian's successor, Constantine, consolidated this move and also declared Christianity the state religion in 315 AD.

While Constantinople thrived, Rome and the Western Empire went into decline. By the fifth century Barbarians had been crossing the frontiers and raiding the Empire for a good many years and the ongoing instability this produced led finally to the sacking of Rome in 410 by Alaric the Visigoth. Thus ended nearly a thousand years of imperial Rome.

For a time the Western Empire was ruled by the Ostrogoths, but a century later the Eastern Emperor Justinius struck back and by 552 had reconquered most of what had been lost. Over the next few centuries, with the Emperor in far-away Constantinople, the Church and its bishops emerged as the principle governing power in what was left of the Western Empire.

The Holy Roman Empire

In the years that followed the Franks from Gaul spread through Italy and became such an important force that in 800 Pope Leo III (the *de facto* ruler of Rome) crowned their king, Charlemagne, Holy Roman Emperor. The concept of the Holy Roman Empire was a strange alliance of temporal and spiritual powers which, despite its strangeness, worked satisfactorily at first.

After the death of Otto III in 1002 the Pope started to assert his power against that of the Emperor and the resulting conflict meant that for hundreds of years Italy was divided between *ghibellines* (supporters of the Emperor) and *guelphs* (supporters of the Pope).

The Papacy gradually increased its power, and by the 13th century Rome was the administrative centre of the Roman Catholic Church and still a formidable political and economic power in its own right. However, while this was happening, northern Italy was becoming a collection of city states which were only very loosely bound by the Holy Roman Empire. As the struggle raged between the two universal leaders, the Pope and the Emperor, their power grew less and less. The city states developed their own government and administrations and increasingly went their own ways.

During the fourteenth century, the leaders of the Holy Roman Empire gradually despaired of ever bringing Italy back under proper control and so withdrew to the German part of the Empire, leaving the peninsula to itself.

The Renaissance and foreign intervention

By the mid-fifteenth century Italy was divided between the Kingdom of Naples (all of southern Italy), by now under Aragon dominion, the Papal States (in the centre), the Duchy of Milan, and the republics of Florence and Venice.

It was this situation which eventually saw the Renaissance flourish especially in Italy, where the little states and principalities, by now fairly prosperous, all tried to outdo each other in art and culture.

Despite their economic and cultural success, the regional Italian states were small, and politically weak next to the giant powers of Spain, France and the Austria of the Hapsburgs. Austria and Spain united under Charles V Hapsburg and fought France for control of Italy. When they made peace in 1559, most of the territory was under Spanish (Hapsburg) control, with the rest French. Only Venice and the Papal States remained independent.

Around this time, when borders remained more or less fixed for well over a century, there were two major events influencing political and economic life: the Reformation which was sweeping northern Europe and causing a great deal of worry to the Papacy; and economic recession, which had hit many Italian cities as the new ocean trade routes started to leave them behind.

At the beginning of the eighteenth century, Spain lost most of Italy to Austria, although through some political machinations the Spanish Bourbons soon regained Naples and Sicily. In the north, economic and industrial advances were made under the Austrians' autocratic rule and this further enhanced the growing divide between the north and the south, which was still almost entirely agricultural.

Napoleon appeared on the scene in 1796, and by 1810 he was in control of the whole peninsula. Among the benefits which his rule brought to the region were the further reduction of the power of the Papacy and the introduction of elected, representative government.

Unification

The drive for a united Italy, which began as soon as Napoleon's armies left the north, and Austria's took their place, has been given the name *Risorgimento* by historians. There were frequent uprisings in many Italian cities during the first half of the nineteenth century, and while they occurred primarily to protest against perceived injustices committed by rulers (principally the Austrians and Bourbons), they increasingly showed a desire to oust the occupiers and set up a free, Republican nation state.

Giuseppe Mazzini was one of the most influential ideologues of Republicanism and his ideas struck a chord in enough hearts to make his dream eventually come true. When unification did come about, it was more like an annexation of territories by the northern kingdom of Piedmont than the free uniting of the Italian peoples. Making a deal with Napoleon III of France, Piedmont's prime minister, Count Camillo Cavour, started a war with Austria, and with French help grabbed most of the northern lands. Tuscany and Emilia–Romagna then ejected their Austrian rulers and added themselves to 'greater Piedmont' forming the nucleus of the Italian state.

Garibaldi, another hero of the period, took troops south to capture Sicily and Naples from the Bourbons. This he quickly did, handing them over to Cavour and the Piedmont king, Vittorio Emanuele, in October 1860. In 1861 the component parts then declared themselves the 'Kingdom of Italy'. Rome and Venice were added in 1871.

Italy's first century

Soon after unification Italy started an attempt at colonial expansion, which led to some bloody and only partially successful escapades in Abysinnia and Eritrea. In 1912 it seized Libya and the Dodecanese Islands from the Turks.

When Italy entered the first world war in 1915, it was largely in order to gain north-eastern territories which were considered by many to be rightfully Italian. Three years of increasingly unpopular warfare finally brought about the victory of Vittorio Veneto, by which Italy gained Trieste, Gorizia and Trentino-Alto Adige.

Immediately after the war, the country became obsessed with the threat of Communist revolution, and it was by exploiting this fear that in 1921 Mussolini and the Fascists were elected to 35 seats in parliament. Using squads of marauding 'black-shirts' as frighteners, Mussolini forced king and parliament to allow him to head and form his own government. In 1925 he became dictator. His strong and autocratic rule, while severely inhibiting individual freedom, did bring some benefits: it introduced heavy-handed but at least workable public institutions; it brought the Mafia to its knees; and it effected a truce (the Lateran Pact) with the Church. The Church had been fuming ever since it had had most of its lands taken away in the unification.

The year 1935 saw another colonial strike into the horn of Africa, and the forming of the Italian East African Empire. When Italy entered the second world war with Nazi Germany, however, it found itself totally unprepared. The war was a military disaster, with heavy losses, especially on the Russian front. By 1943 the writing was on the wall: the Allies were advancing up the peninsula and there was nothing anyone could do. Mussolini was overthrown, but managed to hang on till 1945, defiantly forming the tiny Republic of Salò in the north-east. In the closing months of the war he was captured by partisans. They executed him and strung up his corpse next to that of his lover in Milan's Piazza Loreto.

POLITICS

The Italian political system is currently in a state of turmoil. There are a variety of reasons for this, but two of the most important are undoubtedly the end of the Cold War and the apparently never-ending series of corruption scandals.

Since the end of the last war, the political system has been geared to keeping the Communists out of power. With the end of the Cold War, Communism is no longer seen as a threat and the people who supported the other parties in order to preserve the *status quo* now want the faults in the system addressed.

One of the greatest faults in the post-war system was the corruption it tolerated. It seems that all parties were guilty to a certain extent and, as more and more 'pillars of the establishment' are exposed, there is a widespread disgust among the populace for everything connected with the old order.

Another problem was the electoral system, which was proportional representation in its purest form. It gave seats in parliament to any party which could muster 1% or 2% of the votes. While this was undoubtedly very fair, in practice it has meant that small parties have proliferated and no one party has ever achieved an absolute majority. As a result, government has been grossly inefficient at times. Even general elections failed to change the basic set-up, which had the *Democrazia Cristiana* (DC) ensconced in power from the start.

Commentators abroad and in Italy have talked of a revolution as fundamental as those in Eastern Europe. Indeed, the average Italian is more interested in politics now than at any time since 1968.

In the March 1994 general election, in reaction against the discredited regimes of the Christian Democrats and Socialists, the make-up of the Chamber of Deputies changed dramatically. The *Forza Italia*, headed by tycoon Silvio Berlusconi, became the largest single party in the Italian parliament. The most surprising fact about this is that Berlusconi had entered politics only four months earlier. The Freedom Alliance, a right-wing coalition comprising Berlusconi's own party, the populist *Lega del Nord* (Northern League), and the neo-Fascist MSI, achieved a landslide victory, winning 366 of the 630 seats in the *Camera del Deputati* (Chamber of Deputies).

Aside from the new, free-market oriented *Forza Italia*, a few of the many other parties are described briefly below.

Democrazia Cristiana (now renamed Partito Popolare). This is the party which, until 1994, dominated every Italian government since the war. It covers a wide range of political sentiment from hard right to soft left, united only by a professed Catholicism. It has many factions which very rarely see eye to eye. Only on social matters like divorce and abortion does it find some coherence (in opposing them).

Partito Democratico della Sinistra. This is the rump of the recently disbanded Communist party. It has retained basically the same stance as before, changing name in response to the apparent eclipse of world Communism. In fact, the Italian Communists were never anything like as hard-line as their Soviet namesakes and the new 'Democratic Left' has abandoned even the hammer and sickle which used to appear on its flag. Its vote held up quite well in the 1994 election and it ended up the second largest party in parliament.

Partito Socialista Italiano. The Italian Socialists are socialists only in name. If this is anything at all it is a centre party, but under the leadership of Bettino Craxi (since arrested on corruption charges) it lost all ideological pretensions and become simply a vehicle to power. Despite a terrible reputation for corruption, over the years it scored well in elections, and managed, until 1994, to wield a good deal of governmental power.

Lega del Nord. Led by Umberto Bossi, the Northern League continually rails against Roman mismanagement and southern corruption. It seeks some form of separation for the north from the rest of Italy. At its most moderate it wants a federal solution and at its most extreme it wants a completely separate identity for the northern regions. As part of the Freedom Alliance (see above), it approximately doubled its number of seats in the 1994 election.

Rifondazione Communista. This is the other part of the former Communist party which refused to be part of the new *Partito Democratico della Sinistra.*

Movimento Sociale Italiano. This is the neo-Fascists party, formed shortly after the war. It merged in the late 1970s with the *Destra Nazionale*, thus becoming MSI-DN. As part of the Freedom Alliance (see above), it became the third largest party in parliament after the 1994 election. Now known as *Alleanza Nazionale.*

THE ECONOMY

Throughout the 1980s Italy enjoyed quite brilliant economic growth. It now sees itself as the world's fifth economic power, and although a certain amount of figure-juggling was necessary to bring about this result, it is undoubtedly one of the most adaptable and resilient economies in Europe.

Its performance is still slowed, however, by the backward south, which according to many northerners soaks up much of their hard-earned cash. It is also hampered by an outrageously bloated state sector which pays too many people too much money for too little. Nevertheless, state industry functions remarkably well, given that most of its leaders were appointed for political reasons. It is in the ministries and government offices where the rot really lies. Many are absurdly overmanned, and inadequate controls mean that absenteeism is rife.

Italy's economy is divided between massive companies partly or completely controlled by the state (Fiat, Olivetti, ENEL, ENI) and thousands of tiny, family-based businesses. In the current climate of high interest rates, labour unrest and political instability, it is the latter which are bound to suffer. If too many of these small businesses go under there are no middle-sized ones to keep the economy afloat. What is more, punitive taxation means that there is no carrot for small firms to become bigger. Promises to alleviate these problems helped Berlusconi achieve his stunning victory in the 1994 election.

To be fair, the previous government had been trying to streamline the state sector and it had also talked a good deal about privatizing national industries in an attempt to make them more competitive. But progress has been slow and a national debt exceeding GDP along with a budget deficit at 12% and rising have done little to promote confidence abroad.

This is unfortunate, because to have any hope of convincing the European Union that it is fit to re-enter the Exchange Rate Mechanism, and that monetary union is possible, Italy will have to sort these problems out fast. The devaluation of the Lira at the end of 1992 was the inevitable result of letting the world see that the economy was not being strictly controlled.

CHARACTER AND LIFESTYLE

The dangers of trying to describe the character of a nation are self-evident and, to do the subject justice, far more than these few pages would be necessary. In this section then I will limit myself to discussing a few aspects which have struck me over the years as being relevant to the concerns of this book. What follows is simply a selection of personal thoughts and observations, which may or may not correspond to the way you will eventually see Italy and its people.

Italians and foreigners

Few foreigners end up having a bad time in Italy. Italians have very little of the fierce nationalism of some other European nations and traditionally welcome foreigners with open arms. In the past one of the reasons for this was Italy's low view of itself and its standing with the rest of the world. For a long time seen as the poor men of Europe, with the embarrassment of the war and a grossly inefficient state system, few Italians felt wildly proud of their nationality. In consequence, their treatment of foreigners was at times coloured by a certain amount of envy. Visitors from Northern Europe or other technically advanced countries were apt to find themselves playing the role of minor celebs, popular and respected simply for being foreign. This was always secondary, however, to the straightforward friendly interest which Italians have always shown to outsiders and probably always will.

> During the break in one of the first few lessons of a course, one of my students asked me where I was from. When I said I was English, there was widespread disbelief. Immediately I was informed that I was a very unusual Englishman because I laughed and joked around sometimes.
>
> *Sam Surl (UK)*

The Italian character has not changed, but in the last decade their self-appreciation has received a great boost. The *sorpasso* (overtaking) which took them to fifth place in the table of economic powers, winning the World Cup in soccer, and the success of 'Made in Italy' designer culture have all contributed to the fact that being Italian is 'cool' after all.

A recent survey showed that now over 50% of Italians think that their country is the best place in the world to live. This is symptomatic of the generally buoyant mood which makes Italians envy foreigners considerably less than they used to. A common remark from an Italian in conversation with a foreigner is: '*Però, si sta bene in Italia, non?*' ('Life's good in Italy, isn't it?') and this will invariably be followed by a list of points in its favour – sun, food, attractive men/women, style in general.

Another reason why Italians are less ecstatically xenophile nowadays is because, as the country's world image has improved, so increasing numbers of immigrants have made homes there. While the UK, France and Germany have a certain amount of experience with African and Asian immigrants, Italy has only recently become a popular destination for them and so their presence is causing shock waves and not infrequent displays of racism.

Italians like to see themselves as representative of Latin culture and temperament. They contrast themselves primarily with the Anglo-Saxon, who they see personified in the British. According to the common view they, the Italians, are warm, open and friendly, while the British are cold, insular and reserved; they have the good weather and terrible public services, '*Gli Inglesi*' have the reverse. This is clearly an oversimplification, but in the end it is perhaps not too inaccurate.

Because of the perceived contrast between the two cultures, there is a certain fascination for the Anglo-Saxon (you will frequently hear talk of 'self-control', with the stress on 'con', as if it is a strange and mysterious gift that all English speakers unfailingly possess).

Family

To many people from Anglo-Saxon backgrounds the importance of the family in Italian life seems excessive. A large number of children still continue to live at home until they marry and even when they do not, their lives seem to be organized around it. What is more, there is generally far more of it than a British person, for example, might expect. Cousins, nephews, nieces, aunts, uncles, in-laws even, are all considered immediate family and they manage to get together frequently (with a family that size there is frequently a wedding or Christening or funeral to go to). In some parts of the country it is still possible to find the whole of an extended family living within shouting distance of each other.

Even when young people move away for work, they frequently travel back home at the weekend to rejoin the family unit. Being in constant contact with home, and when possible being in close physical proximity to the family, is a psychological necessity for many Italians and problems of privacy and independence tend to be of secondary importance.

Possibly as a result of this, Italians seem to suffer relatively little from the problems of alienation and loneliness which are common in the English-speaking world. But there is also a flip-side. While Italian families stick together through thick and thin, this can be at the expense of the state and any other form of authority. The lack of credence given to central government, especially in the south, is probably due to the fact that in the past it has rarely been there when they have needed it, and so families have had to take care of themselves and in ways not always entirely lawful. The Mafia started as a self-help group organized by Sicilian peasants who could not rely on the state to safeguard their land and possessions. They call themselves 'the family' and demand absolute loyalty. While there is no question of every Italian family being a mini-Mafia, it is true to say that a high degree of solidarity is required from all members, and if you can ever help your own blood you are expected to do so without question.

Youth

It is easy to dismiss Italian youth as spoilt and incapable of looking after itself. Indeed it is true that many young men have no idea about how to go about washing clothes, cooking and cleaning the house, but this ignorance has come about because of several factors which are far less marked in Anglo-Saxon society. For a start, the housing situation in Italy is such that there is very little accommodation available for young people who want to be independent. Another factor is that the state gives virtually no financial help to the unemployed, so unless children find steady well-paid employment they are economically dependent on their parents. Even when at university there are no government grants, so, again, the parents have to pay for everything. All this, together with high unemployment and the relatively high cost of living, make living at home by far the most practical solution.

Another important fact pointed out by sociologists is that children are becoming rarer in Italy. The average number of children per family is now less than two and it seems that, like all rare commodities, they are valued all the more. Given the economic prosperity which Italy has found since the war, parents are in a position to give their children 'everything which they never had', and in doing so they get a good deal of satisfaction. At its most extreme, this phenomenon produces fat kids with flash cars and mountains of designer clothes. In more general terms, it means that Italian youth can appear overly protected and 'spoilt' by parents.

Bella figura and being stylish

This is one of the central themes in Italian culture and you will come across it more or less wherever you are and with whomever you are dealing. Literally *Bella figura* means 'pretty face' and it denotes the importance of appearances and of making the right impression. This can be through clothes, cars, lifestyle, behaviour – anything in fact which can be observed and judged by other people.

Rather than aiming for *bellezza* as the name suggests, it is usually designed to indicate wealth. Beauty and elegance come second, or, rather, they are often synonymous with wealth. Presumably this is why designer labels became so important in Italy – they are the equivalent of an expensive price-tag.

One of the reasons for this preoccupation with demonstrating wealth is surely the fact that a large part of the population can still remember what it was like before Italy became relatively prosperous. As kids, economic hardship prevented many of them from seeing much glamour, and everything they had was functional rather than decorative. It is easy to see how the arrival of money in many households has turned priorities upside down.

Second, it is important to consider that the Italians are a highly 'visual' race. Look at the architecture of the great cities, or the uniforms of the police, if you need evidence of this. The fact is that what things (and people) look like matters intensely to Italians, sometimes more than anything else. Hardly anybody, it seems, bothers with seat-belts, and the most important reason is that they do not fit in with the image that people want to create behind the wheel – ie casual, unconcerned style.

Regionalism

Despite a growing pride in Italian-ness, many people still feel a far stronger bond with their town or village of origin than with the nation as a whole. When two Italians meet, one of the first questions is 'Where are you from?' and this piece of information is incredibly important in the mental categorizing which then goes on.

Each region, has a series of characteristics attached to it which conventional wisdom accepts without question. There are, indeed, huge differences between some regions of Italy, in terms of customs, dialect and even mentality. This is hardly surprising when you consider that Italy as a precise geographic entity is not much more than a century old. Its elongated shape too has meant that for a long time contact between north and south has been minimal. The media have also played a role in establishing regional stereotypes and thus influencing how people define themselves.

The fact that Italians are usually proud of where they come from means that rivalry is inevitable – and it is not just between regions. In some of the more rural areas, you often find that people in neighbouring villages cannot stand each other and recount stories about the vices of their 'enemy' to anyone who will listen. Supposedly 'friendly' football matches can turn into highly emotional affairs in which the honour of the whole population is at stake.

On a much larger scale, there is a deep rift in Italy between the north and the south. Northerners call southerners *Terroni* – literally 'earth people', implying that they are all peasants, uneducated, lazy and corrupt. This last charge has recently been seen to be hypocritical as there have been as many 'rake-off' scandals in Milan as in Naples.

Southerners, on the other hand, term their compatriots from the north *Polentoni* (referring to a common northern dish) and tend to view them as cold, unfriendly workaholics who are obsessed with punctuality and regulations.

It is the south that comes out of the confrontation worst. It is consistently attacked for being industrially backward (which is true) and for draining the resources of the north. The anti-south feeling has now crystallized in a growing *Lega del Nord* which would like to cast off the south and become a major European player.

I was driving down a busy street in Rome when suddenly all the cars in front of me suddenly screeched to a halt. There was a pause of a good thirty seconds before a cyclist came past, dodged through the waiting cars and went on her way. Immediately all the cars shot off again. As I was going past the place where I assumed the block must have been, I noticed a black cat slinking away. Later I found out that a black cat crossing your path is terribly bad luck. Presumably all the car drivers had waited till the cyclist came along and took the bad luck, before going on.

Tracey Davis (USA)

Religion

Despite the fact that the focal point of world Catholicism is in their capital, Italians are a surprisingly irreligious lot. To be more precise, indifference is by far the most common religious position and while a majority would say they believed in God or 'something', the Church serves mainly for births, weddings and deaths. The rest of the time it receives relatively little attention. Having said that, the effect of Catholic morals on everyday living is still felt. In hospitals, government offices and millions of homes, crucifixes and Madonnas are common fixtures, bearing witness to religion's continuing, albeit fading, presence in the fabric of society.

While it may appear that religious feeling is stronger in the South, in fact it is more often pagan superstition subsumed by official Catholicism. Death is a taboo subject, rather like sex, and Italians have a more direct, emotional relationship with both, than do many Northern Europeans. It is difficult to say whether the Church is directly responsible for this or not. In any case it seems a common formula in many Latin (and therefore almost always Catholic) countries.

Cleanliness

If cleanliness is next to Godliness, Italians must be the holiest of the Europeans. While some Italian cities are undeniably filthy, when you get away from public spaces and into the private, personal domain, Italians are scrupulously, some would say obsessively, clean. They buy more detergents than any other country in Europe and every house has a washing machine.

If you walk into an Italian home, the lady of the house will always say '*Scusa il disordine!*' ('Sorry about the mess!') despite the fact that invariably everything you can see is perfectly tidy and spotlessly clean. To be seen out in clothes which have not just been cleaned and ironed is almost a crucifiable offence. One of the reasons why youth fashions like punk never really caught on here is that it is anathema for Italians to draw attention to clothes which are ragged and not very clean.

Partly, this is all to do with *bella figura* (see above) but it is not just on the surface. Personal hygiene is as thorough as what you can see. Showers are taken at the very least once a day, and in summer more often. One thing which really astounds most Italians is that in the UK, for example, bidets are not common bathroom fixtures. Their first reaction is one of disbelief, and finally a mixture of bewilderment and disgust. This fact, along with a less rigid dress code, means that foreigners, and especially the British, are often seen as definitely lacking in this area.

Corruption and *abusivismo*

Being infinitely corruptible is part of the media stereotype of the Italian and indeed corruption is apparent almost anywhere you look in modern Italian society. The *Tangentopoli* scandals which dominated 1993 were only the uncovering of a phenomenon which everybody knew existed. Paying bribes (*tangenti*) to government ministers for public works contracts is par for the course, and no shopkeeper in Naples or Palermo seriously thinks he or she can avoid paying money (*pizzo*) to the Cammorra and Mafia protection rackets.

If corruption is an undeniable part of life, so too is *abusivismo*. This is the practice of ignoring or getting round the law, either for money or simply to avoid hassle. Eight million houses and 14 million apartments do not officially exist in Italy because they were built without planning permission, and tax evasion is so widespead that officials reckon they get less than one quarter of what is owed to them.

Despite all this, it is plain silly to assert (as even some Italians do) that a tendency to be dishonest is in the blood. The reasons are at least six-fold:

- The old electoral system gave too much power to the parties.
- A history of weak and ineffectual government does little to encourage respect for authority.
- The philosophy of looking after yourself (and 'family') is widespread and influential.
- Italian culture nurtures a natural streetwise business sense, or an 'eye' for a deal.
- The bureacratic system is so full of red tape regulations that it encourages people to find other ways to get what they want.
- There is the traditional Catholic indulgence to wrong-doers.

The third and forth of these are probably a result of the first and second. If they are, it is clear that the recent change in the electoral system is of vital importance to the future of the country.

The proportional representation system, which existed until recently, meant that most parties got a share of the power. Different areas of public administration were unofficially assigned to different parties, and jobs were handed out to people of the right political colour by a process known as *lotizzazione*. This will undoubtedly go on for a long time to come, as will the system of *raccommandazzioni*, whereby all other jobs are given out through personal connections and string-pulling for favours.

Of course it is impossible to predict with any certainty, but if the general public could see the end of phenomena such as *lotizza-zione* and *raccommandazioni*, maybe some civic sense of responsibility would develop. As things stand, nobody plays by the rules, for two reasons: first because it's impossible – the rules are too many, too complicated and too arbitrary; and second, and perhaps most fundamentally, because nobody is going to stop cheating the system while they can see that everyone else is doing the same.

In the meantime, Italians are dubious about the so-called 'revolution' which foreign journalists see happening in their political class. It will take a lot to convince ordinary Italians that the state and the system are worthy of their respect. Until that happens they will continue to ignore one-way signs when there are no traffic police, and keep their 'friends in high places'.

ESSENTIAL SIGNS AND GESTURES

Italians are renowned for speaking as much with their hands as with their mouths, and to follow a conversation a knowledge of the common signs and gestures is very helpful. The following are some of the most frequently used and, while they may be difficult to visualize from the description, once you have seen them they are all very simple.

Money. To indicate money people often rub the first two fingers against the thumb.

Ma che dici. This is the gesture which is often used to caricature Italians. It is made by holding your hand out, palm up, with the fingers and thumb pointing up and touching at the tips. By moving your hand back and forth in this position you demonstrate disbelief and a desire to contradict. It corresponds to something like 'What are you talking about?' in English.

Hands together as if in prayer. This can have a similar meaning to the above, but it also has a sense of exhorting or begging someone to do something. Students who do not want homework might well use this.

There aren't/isn't any. This is a very useful signal, used to imply a lack of whatever you are talking about. The thumb and forefinger are extended from the fist which is rotated sideways from the wrist.

Steal/stealing/stolen. Start with you hand open and curl the fingers in, starting with the little one at the bottom.

Very good. The gesture can refer to anybody or anything and is done by rubbing the thumb nail down the lower jaw bone.

Very good (food). With reference to food, the index finger pointing into the cheek and twisting round means that something is exceptionally good. This is a winner if you are invited to someone's house for dinner.

Go away/escape. This is not used to tell somebody to 'get lost', but simply to refer to the action of going away in the past, present or future. The left palm (facing down) is struck once or twice by the side of the right hand. In a bar somebody might do this, after pointing to themselves to indicate their intention to leave.

Papera. For some reason ducks are considered stupid in Italy, and so young people sometimes make a duck out of their forearm and hand to bate each other.

All of the above can be used effectively by a newcomer to Italy without risk of causing offence. The gestures which follow are just as common, but can give offence if used in the wrong situation. It is probably best not to use them at all until you are very proficient in the language.

Very bad/strong dislike. This is an expression of personal antipathy and is offensive when referred to an individual. The finger tips start at the Adam's apple and move up and out from under the chin.

Cornuto. This means 'horned' literally and refers to the horns which supposedly grow on a cuckold's forehead. It is one of the most common insults, presumably because it represents one of the Italian male's greatest fears. The gesture is a clenched fist with the forefinger and little finger extended like horns.

Culo rotto. This is a rather vulgar gesture made with the forefingers and thumbs extended, and the hands held a few inches apart. It is used when a person is considered lucky, or sometimes as a playful threat of physical violence.

Che palle. Hands a little below the waist, as if holding two heavy balls. It is normally accompanied by sighs of '*Che palle!*' ('What a drag!') and indicates boredom and frustration.

Part 3

TEACHING ENGLISH
TO ITALIANS

8 | The Italian education system

Italian children usually start school at the age of five or six. The law obliges them to stay at school until they finish middle school at about fourteen years-old. After that they are free to leave and find a job, if they choose. This tends to happen more in the south than in the north, but in general the majority continue their education at least until the end of secondary school, which they finish at the age of eighteen or nineteen. Then about 40% of students go on to university. Students can take more-or-less as long as they want to complete their degrees, but it is rare to take fewer than four years and seven or eight years is by no means unusual.

The basic stages in the education system are as follows:

- 6–11 *Scuola Elementare* (primary/elementary)
- 11–14 *Scuola Media* (middle)
- 14–19 *Scuola Secondaria Superiore* (secondary/high)
- 19– *university*

Despite some black spots, Italian schools compare well with the rest of Europe, and most English-speakers with any knowledge or experience of the system agree that Italian kids work harder than they did at school. Unlike in the UK, where the last two years of study are limited to three subjects, in Italy they have a broader range all through secondary school and the subjects are studied in considerable depth. However, by going to *Scuola Superiore*, students are already orienting themselves in a certain direction through the choice of school they make. They can choose from *liceo classico*, *liceo scientifico*, *liceo artistico*, and *liceo linguistico* if they want a traditionally academic school. The technical schools offer a more vocational approach and they are known as: *istituto commerciale*, *istituto industriale*, *istituto agrario*, and *istituto nautico*. There are also teacher-training schools. All of these teach the same core subjects plus those relevant to the appropriate type of school.

At the last count there were more than a million students in Italian universities and many are hopelessly overcrowded. This means that most studying is done alone with very little guidance from professors. While the system may have advantages in terms of independence and self-discipline, it means that a student trying to get to grips with a language, for example, is very limited in what he or she can do to improve practical skills.

The teaching of English

Until very recently languages were not taught in schools before the *Scuola Media*, but they are now being introduced in the latter stages of *Scuola Elementare* too. In theory there is a choice of four modern languages at school (French, German, Spanish and English). However, usually English and French predominate, and as English becomes increasingly ubiquitous in professional life it is gaining the upper hand over French.

The result is that school-leavers can have up to eight years of *inglese scolastico* behind them, but, as they often point out, this does not mean that they are capable of stringing two words together. Given the grammar/translation approach which most state schools take, this is hardly surprising.

At university English is a component part of many degree courses, but because of the excessive numbers and because courses often require students only to read, skills such as speaking and listening can remain at a very low level.

Christine Wood (Lettrice, University of Salerno) summarizes the situation as follows:

English, along with other languages is offered in all Italian universities, either as the main subject of study or as an adjunct to other courses. Because of its evergrowing international importance it is being made obligatory in more and more degree courses, and an optional in most others.However since universities are didactically autonomous, the degree structures depend upon the individual faculties and what the students decide to specialise in. For this reason there is very little uniformity nationwide.

The content of the language/literature/translation course is at the discretion of the university lecturer and his assistants (*lettori*) and so varies a good deal. What is more, it is not always directly relevant to the degree the students are taking. More often than not, course content depends on the background, interests and publications of the lecturer himself; this can mean that students end up buying and studying the books he has written. There is also no standardisation amongst universities about the levels of language ability which students must reach in order to pass their exams. At the end of the day all this simply means that a lot of people study a lot of English and a lot of the time still are not very good.

9 | Italians as students

Italians in the classroom, like Italians everywhere, are warm, responsive and willing to give of themselves. In short, they are a lot of fun to teach.

In some respects they are no different from students the world over, and parts of this chapter could be equally well applied to any nationality. There are, however, a few characteristics which differentiate them and some comments may legitimately be made which may prove useful to anyone coming to Italy to teach.

Expectations

It is an obvious but important fact that most Italians have been through (or are going through) the Italian education system. As a result, their expectations are to a large extent determined by what happened in the language classroom at school. This may or may not be a problem , depending on the circumstances and individuals concerned. Older students, for example, sometimes have difficulty in adapting their learning strategies to different methods.

Many language schools now adopt what is vaguely called the 'Communicative' approach, which concentrates more on the spoken word and less on the traditional diet of grammar and translation. Given the contrast, it is not surprising that the first time students are exposed to speaking practice in closed pairs there is sometimes a degree of shock and even resistance. Usually gentle cajoling and reasoned argument win the day, but if they do not it is up to the teacher to decide how much he or she is willing to modify his or her way of teaching to what the students want. It may be that pushing on regardless invokes so much ill will that it becomes counter-productive to learning.

Another expectation which teachers come across frequently is one most probably connected to the type of society in which Europeans live. It is the idea that to learn English a student need only pay the money and come to the lessons, where the teacher will pour the language into his or her head, a certain amount each lesson. Many students become frustrated and some even angry when at the end of a course or series of lessons they still cannot speak fluent English. Basically this problem arises for two main reasons: first, many people underestimate the time and effort needed to master a language; and, second, it is not always clear to students that passive knowledge and understanding do not bring with them an ability to produce language spontaneously – ie to speak. This needs time and patience and the use of activities or exercises with which the students may be unfamiliar, and which they will possibly find intimidating to begin with.

Like much of what is in this chapter, this fact is not usually something you can change. All you can do is be aware and so, in a sense, prepared.

Teacher–student relationship

The expectations discussed above also have an important bearing on the way students view you, the teacher. In state schools everywhere teachers are in a position to dictate every aspect of the lessons. Their place in the accepted hierarchy, their age and their knowledge of their subject all ensure unquestioned authority. The case of the English teacher outside the established education system is strikingly different: it is very likely that you will not have the seniority in years to command respect, and despite the fact that you are a 'teacher' you are not automatically entitled to the same powers that a state school teacher enjoys. These differences make it almost certainly a mistake to try to play the traditional school master or mistress. Probably the best relationship to aim for is a fraternal one – one where you direct without being authoritarian and help without being superior.

In the school where I worked in Rome we had a lot of nuns studying English. When there was a strike by the cigarette manufacturers, nobody could get cigarettes except on the black market at ridiculously high prices. The strike had been going for about a week and I was desperate for a decent cigarette, not one of the horrible roll-ups I had been making with pipe tobacco. After one lesson, one of my nuns took me aside and, after rummaging in her bag, produced two packets of Marlboro. She gave them to me with a smile and a pat on the back, saying that I was a *bravo ragazzo*.

Bill Hetherington (USA)

One of the effects of this open type of relationship is that students will express their feelings more freely, and this includes dissatisfaction. Italians are not the most reticent of people, and they will not waste much time telling you if they do not like what you are asking them to do. Of course this can be very discouraging, and sometimes it may be simply laziness on their part, but still it should push you to find stimulating, useful activities for your students. As long as students can see why they are doing a particular activity or exercise, they will generally cooperate. Problems arise when they think that something is a waste of time.

It is important, then, to make the point of what they are doing clear. By explaining the *why* as well as the *what*, you demonstrate that you do not expect them to do something just because teacher says so.

The Italian way

There are some Italian tendencies which can be disturbing for teachers encountering them for the first time. Punctuality, for example, has never been a big hit in Italy. For many students the idea that a lesson should begin when it is timetabled to begin may seem strange. For them it would seem more sensible to wait until most people have arrived. There is not a lot you can do about this; time is a more fluid concept in Italy and the onus is on you as the foreigner to fit in. Try to encourage people to be on time, certainly, but do not be too surprised or cross when they are not.

Another thing which may surprise a green teacher is how much Italians like talking. Italians are great talkers, and there is nothing they like better than a good argument. Often it takes very little to spark off a loud discussion of something you consider a long way from the point of the lesson. Once again a certain amount of tolerance is in order here because you cannot expect your students to stop being Italian for the couple of hours when they come to your lesson.

Generally, they are also keen to form some sort of personal bond with the teacher, to break down the formality of the situation.

Italians tend to have an innate lack of respect for figures of authority and you will often find yourself being drawn away from your lesson towards aimless chit-chat. Be friendly by all means, but be firm too. This is very difficult sometimes and you need to be patient, but you must do it – otherwise your lesson will fall to pieces.

Finally, a word about testing. At some point or other you will have to test your students. Creating the right conditions for a test can be quite a battle. Italians often seem unable to resist the temptation to cheat in tests and exams, and sometimes resent the fact that you try to stop them. The concept of working alone, without help, is apparently quite alien. Maybe it has something to do with the corruption which Italians see at every level of society, maybe it is the idea that 'it's not what you know, but who you know' – whatever the cause, be prepared, do not turn your back for a minute and make the conditions absolutely clear right from the start.

Speaking English

Italians, like all Latin people, are blessed with a highly com-municative temperament. They will generally speak freely and without inhibitions about anything, from their own feelings and emotions to the price of spaghetti. They have no qualms about expressing an opinion or disagreeing with someone else's. In short they have in their nature the desire to communicate, which is what language learning is all about.

While this natural volubility is undoubtedly a big bonus when it comes to getting students to speak, it does have a negative side. They are so used to simply opening their mouths and having language fall out that when this does not happen (when they try to speak English), they can get very frustrated and will frequently give up without giving it their best shot.

Another common result is that when a discussion starts to take off, students get so carried away with their ideas and what they want to say, they forget that they are meant to be talking in English. At this point you have the unpleasant duty of being a complete wet blanket. You have to remind everyone patiently that they are in an English lesson and thus destroy the momentum of the discussion.

The fear of making mistakes, common to almost all language learners, is another factor which impedes Italians. This is partly due to the central role given to grammar in the traditional teaching of languages, and partly due to the simple fact that nobody likes being wrong or, worse, being seen to be wrong. Character plays a substantial role here, but in general most Italians will 'have a go' if they can see that nobody is going to mock their efforts.

For more practical ideas of how to get students talking in English, see Chapter 10, under 'Four skills – speaking'.

Slipping into Italian

In any monolingual teaching, especially at lower levels, there is an understandable tendency to slip into the mother-tongue. You will have to decide how far you want to take the 'no Italian' rule, and it will obviously vary from level to level. One thing to be aware of is that if you start using Italian, even in inconsequential asides, you are legitimizing the very thing you are otherwise doing everything you can to discourage.

Among the students themselves, it is inevitable and not always undesirable that some Italian will be used. In low-level pairwork, for instance, it can be productive for one student to explain something to another in his or her own language, as long as in the process they do not lose sight of the point of the exercise – an information gap activity or role play which slides into Italian is clearly useless.

To get a group of people who all share one language to speak to each other in another is a difficult task. However, there are a few things you can do to improve the chances of this happening (at least some of the time).

Consensus

At the beginning of the course, try to get a consensus from the class that it is a good idea to speak English wherever possible. This should not be too difficult as most people start language courses with excellent intentions, and will be only too happy to give them some form of public expression. Once the class has agreed to this, they will have to do battle with their consciences as well as with you every time the issue arises. Admittedly, consciences have varying degrees of influence and for some this tactic will be useless – however, it may tip the balance in your favour so it should not be excluded out of hand.

Constant reminders

Have on the wall notices and speech-bubbles containing the most common student demands in English (eg 'What does . . . mean?', 'How do you spell . . .?', etc). When students ask you these questions in Italian you can point to the English versions, getting them to ask you in English, thus showing that they are quite capable of performing simple information exchanges without resorting to Italian. Before long the most common question forms will be known by heart and a substantial victory will have been won.

Clear instructions

Students often feel the need to speak their own language when they are in doubt or when they do not understand what they have to do. For this reason clear instructions to any activity or exercise are vital, and as verbal instructions are confusing at the best of times a physical demonstration is frequently much more helpful. If you can make the mechanics of an activity crystal clear, you remove one source of uncertainty, allowing your students to concentrate fully on using the language you want them to practise.

Emphasize exceptions to the rule

When you are looking at a complex area of grammar it may be that after repeated attempts to convey a concept there is still a great deal of confusion. At this point it is tempting to feel that only a thorough discussion in the students' own language will clarify the situation. If you decide that getting your concept over is more important than staying in English, let students know that this is a rare and temporary occurrence; formally mark it out as a period of Italian, do not let it go on too long, and when it finishes make sure that everyone knows it is finished and that you are returning to the normal (English) mode of communication.

Penalty games

For various reasons you will sometimes find that a class, or some members of it, are still using too much Italian. One of the problems is probably that they do not realize it is happening as much as it is, and so the first thing to do is to make them aware.

One idea often put forward is to have a system whereby every time someone uses Italian they have to put 100 lire (or some such sum) into a box. Whatever is collected is then used for a class night out. In practice this system is difficult to enforce, and tends to be quickly forgotten.

A similar, but slightly more practical approach is to give everyone three rubber-bands at the start of the lesson and announce that for every utterance in Italian they must give you a rubber-band. This arrangement has the advantage that giving up a rubber-band is not as ostensibly a punishment as is the 100 lire fine, and so it all seems less Draconian.

Whatever set-up you use, the point is that students should be made aware of every non-English utterance, in the hope that they then stem the flow of their own accord. Of course this will not work with everyone but if you take it seriously it should have some effect (if you do not, it will not work at all).

10 Methods and ideas

This chapter describes basic teaching methods and offers ideas and suggestions for applying them to Italian learners.

A BASIC TEACHING PARADIGM

A large part of teaching English involves introducing students to new language. In most cases this will take the form of a grammatical structure, a function (eg making invitations) or a lexical set (eg vocabulary of food). Whatever your new language is, to 'teach' it effectively you need to go through a few set stages. Naturally opinions vary on the details of these stages, but there is more or less a consensus on the basic pattern. This is borne out by the fact that the same general model is used by the majority of teacher-training institutes. It looks like this:

(1) Lead-in.
(2) Focus on new language.
(3) Examine form and meaning.
(4) Controlled practice.
(5) Freer practice.

Before looking at each of these stages separately, it is important to point out that lessons should not necessarily contain this system and nothing else. For a variety of reasons it is not always possible for a lesson to take precisely this form. Sometimes you may not want to teach anything explicitly but have a skills-based lesson. In this case new language will crop up intermittently throughout the lesson and you will have to decide whether it is worth spending time on or not.

The guidelines set forth here are intended as just that – guidelines. They are not incontrovertible and the more experienced you are the more you will develop your own views on the best way of doing things.

Finally, it should be said that it is very rare for a teacher to have to devise all the parts of a lesson from scratch. Course books do a lot of the work for you and, as you will see if you glance through any of the most popular textbooks, they usually follow a plan very similar to the one detailed here (for more information on textbooks see Appendix 7).

I am now going to examine each stage individually. Inevitably such a discussion is rather vague and abstract and so I have included at the end some concrete examples to make the ideas clearer.

Lead-in

Your lead-in should serve two main functions:

- It should be a gentle introduction to a language area (and possibly a lesson).
- It should expose your students to the target language in as real a context as possible.

If you do not want to let your students see or hear the language just yet, you should at least create a situation in which the target language would emerge naturally.

The way you go about leading into a subject depends to a certain extent on what exactly you want to teach. The simplest thing to do is to give students something to read or listen to. Alternatively you could start a discussion of something topical or of interest to your students which is connected to your theme. You could tell an anecdote using the language yourself, or you could play a game or do a puzzle which is in some way relevant. The thing to remember is that you are trying to get over an identifiable context for your language, so that the meaning will be clear. Therefore whatever you do should not be very difficult – you do not want anything to distract from the main point of what you are trying to get over to your students.

Focus on language

Now, in some way, you have to home-in on your target language. If the students have it in front of them or have just heard it, you can ask questions to draw their attention to it. If you have only provided the context in your lead-in, you can try to get them to supply the language needed. By trying to elicit the language in this way you also have the chance to see whether or not students are already familiar with it. It might turn out that they are, in which case a detailed examination of the form and meaning may not be necessary and you can therefore move straight on to the practice stage.

Examine form and meaning

At this point you want to be sure that students have a clear idea of what the language means, so you should ask questions to check this. Because this is such a crucial stage in the presentation, you should make sure that you err on the side of caution rather than speed. There are two good reasons for this: students (even Italian ones) may not always feel like telling you when something is not absolutely clear; and people often think they understand before they actually do. So ask three or four 'yes/no' questions even if students seem to have no problems. Questions like 'Do you understand?' are not very useful because if the response is 'Yes' you have only their word for it, and if it is 'No' you still have not got to the heart of the matter. It is really up to you to make sure they understand.

Imagine you are teaching the structure 'I'd like (a coffee)' in a café/bar situation. To check meaning, you could wait for students to respond, eg by miming the action of giving you a coffee. To distinguish between 'I'd like' and the more abrupt/less acceptable 'I want', you might use cards with smiling/unsmiling faces. Clearly, at the level at which you would teach, 'I'd like', students would not have sufficient language to tolerate wordy explanations or any but the most basic questions, so mime and context are very important.

When you have done this, focus on the form and point out any irregularities or things which can be different (the negative and interrogative forms of verb tenses, for example). Again, this would need to be done very simply at low levels.

Controlled practice

There are two parts to this stage. Sometimes one or the other will not be necessary, depending on the proficiency of your class and the difficulty of your teaching point.

The first part is the checking and practising of pronunciation. Give students a clear model and get them to repeat it a few times. This oral repetition of new language, or 'drilling', is often under-valued because it can seem mindless and there is the fear that students might feel stupid doing it. Actually they usually appreciate it because the process of getting their mouths round new words or formulations is not as simple as a native speaker tends to think. You can also make the drilling more interesting by not limiting it to just the whole class repeating in unison ('choral' drilling). Individual drilling will give students the certainty that they are doing it correctly, and 'substitution' drills (changing one or more elements of the model) add variety.

The second part of controlled practice usually takes the form of a fairly straightforward written exercise. A gap-fill or something where there is only one possible answer is most suitable here. It provides a space for the new language to sink in while students look at different examples and work things out for themselves at their own speed.

Freer practice

If you have done everything above people should now be ready to move on to some freer practice. It is time to let go of the reins a little and see what students can do without your breathing down their neck. Give them an activity to do which involves the new language, but which requires other skills as well. In this way what they have just learned slots in nicely alongside the body of language which they already have. Free practice activities can be oral, written or a mixture. They should aim to stimulate students to produce as well as receive language. Communicative 'information gap' activities are ideal at this stage (see p 122). Other possibilities are: making questionnaires and conducting surveys; role-plays; a personalization in the form of a composition or short talk; a discussion; a game. All of these methods are described elsewhere, so I shall not go into them here.

EXAMPLE LESSONS

Example 1 – elementary level

Aim of lesson: to teach 'should' and 'ought to' to a class of elementary students.

As a lead-in, write up a problem of your own on the board. It could be anything at all and it does not matter whether it is true or not. The important thing is to present the class with a situation to which they can relate.

When everyone has understood the problem, ask the class directly for advice ('What should I do?'). If anyone knows the forms 'should' or 'ought to' they may use them now, but the chances are that you will just get half phrases and verbs thrown at you. Write up a list of all the suitable suggestions and then write at the top 'advice' (explain this if necessary). This is to demonstrate exactly what the language you are about to show them is used for. Assuming one of the pieces of advice offered by the class was 'go for a holiday', take that and write up:

(Your name) . . . . . go to Calabria for a holiday.

Point at the space and ask if anyone can supply a suitable word. If someone offers either of the forms you want, write it in and then ask for another possibility. Write this in above the first and indicate that they are equivalents (this may not be true strictly speaking, but for elementary learners it is OK to say so). As a quick meaning check, ask 'Is it necessary to go on holiday?' (no) and 'Is it a good idea?' (yes). As a further check you could ask how they would say the same thing in Italian (*dovresti*).

Then drill the phrase a few times to get the pronunciation right – both 'should' and 'ought' present problems for Italians because for them the letters have very little relation to the sound. The meaning of the new language should be clear by now, but the form will not. You need to indicate that both the forms have the characteristics of modal verbs (for precise information on this, see the chapter on 'Teaching grammar and functions').

At this point students have had quite a lot to take in, so a quiet written exercise will let the information sink in and help clarify any vague ideas. Something like the following is good because it is straightforward and mechanical:

> *Giuseppe has got a Pizzeria in the centre of Rome. But nobody ever goes there. It is cold inside and there is no paint on the walls. Also Giuseppe doesn't know how to make a good pizza and he hasn't got a wood fire. Another problem is that Giuseppe smells. This is because he rarely has a shower. He spends a lot of money on advertising but it doesn't seem to attract people.*

What should Giuseppe do to get people in his pizzeria? Write 5 sentences.

1. He should ....
2. ....
3. ....
4. ....
5. ....

Give students plenty of time to do this and check it thoroughly afterwards. Now is the time that the ideas they will take away with them are being formed, so accuracy is vital.

For less controlled practice, there are several possibilities. You might, for instance, get students to write down two or three problems of their own, which they pass on to their neighbour. The neighbour then thinks up some suitable advice and sends it back. Alternatively, do this orally. You might want to give students a list of problems if they are lacking in imagination.

As an extension of this, you might ask small groups to prepare questionnaires based on 'should/ought to' statements. These might include:

Should old people get pensions?
Should parents know everything about their children?
Should murderers be executed?
Should politicians have immunity from the law?
Should the government be tougher with the Mafia?

Having prepared five or six questions, students interview other members of the class. At the end you could have everyone report their findings. If there is enough interest, you might be able to start a discussion on a few of the questions.

Example 2 – intermediate level

Aim of lesson: to teach conjunctions of time ('as', 'by the time', 'whenever', 'as soon as', 'when', 'while') to a class of good intermediate students.

Students at this level will often already have encountered the language you decide to work on. However, the mere fact that they have seen it before does not mean they will use it correctly and at the right moment. In this presentation students will probably be familiar with words like 'when' and 'while' and they will have few problems using them because there are obvious equivalents in Italian (*quando* and *mentre*). An expression like 'by the time', on the other hand, will probably be new and therefore not so easily assimilated. It occurs less frequently and is difficult to translate accurately.

Start by giving students the following text to read:

> *'I'm going to go and see mum for a few days,' said Margaret Wood as she put a huge plate of egg and chips in front of her even huger husband. 'Good show,' thought Steven reaching for the ketchup, 'I'll have the house to myself.' And he started to plan what he would do as soon as his wife was safely out of the way. By the time he had finished his chips, he had everything clearly sorted out in his mind. He patted his stomach contentedly and smiled happily across the table.*
>
> *At half past two Mrs Wood kissed her husband on the cheek and hurried out to catch her bus. As she walked along she thought about the strange look on her husband's face when she had told him she was going out. What was he planning? He had been behaving rather mysteriously recently, in fact for quite some time now. Whenever she said she was going out, his eyes seemed to light up and sometimes, while they were talking, he just forgot what they were talking about and stared blankly into space. She would have to ask him straight out . . .*
>
> *Meanwhile, Steven Wood was very busy. After making sure*

that his wife had really gone, he locked the front door and went into the study. In the corner of the room was a large square box. It was made of a dark wood and had strange symbols engraved in the sides. He stood and looked at it, watching until he sensed that something inside was coming to life. He had not done this since Margaret had gone to see her mother a week ago. He stood up straight and before stepping forward, he licked his lips in anticipation.

After checking general comprehension of the text you can move onto some more pointed questions aimed at focusing attention on the target language. A question like 'When did Steven's eyes light up' should produce an answer involving 'whenever', and similar questions can be used to extract the other time conjunctions in the text. You can get students to write answers to these, or give them orally, whichever you prefer.

Now you have got the students looking at the words you are interested in, you should move on to explaining the meaning. Do this by asking questions to pinpoint the differences, referring back to the text whenever possible. With the 'whenever' example, the main point is that it refers to an action which happens several times. Point students to the sentence in which it occurs and ask, 'Did this happen once?'. From their reply you will know how much explanation is necessary. Continue in this way, examining and comparing each one, and finally point out that all these words are followed by a subject and a verb. If your students (and you) feel happy with grammatical terms you can say they are conjunctions and need clauses after them.

The controlled practice stage can be a few sentences to complete with the relevant word: For example:

My grandfather was always very generous. . . . . . he came to stay, he brought us presents. *(whenever)*

A slightly less mechanical exercise could involve sentence heads to be completed orally. For example:

By the time the police arrived, ...
As soon as I heard the noise, I . . . . .

For the freer practice stage you could distribute picture stories for the students to write up. By choosing well you can virtually ensure that some of the new words are used. A similar activity could be done with a short video, which then has to be retold. Alternatively you could get students to write an ending to the story they started with. Because this type of language occurs most naturally in writing, it is best to keep the practice written too.

Example 3 – the first lesson

Preparing the first lesson with a new group is always a little worrying: more often than not you know nothing about the people you are going to face and they probably do not know each other either. All this uncertainty means that everyone will be rather nervous. Nevertheless you can use this lack of knowledge as the basis for your lesson.

The following plan can be modified and used for almost any level. I present it here in a fairly simple form, intended for low-level students.

Write your name on the board, introduce yourself and go round asking people their names. Now return to the board, put a question mark next to your name and say 'Question?' in an interrogative tone. Unless everybody in the class is totally without life or intelligence, someone (probably everybody) will come up with 'What's your name?'. Model it, drill it and write it up next to your name.

Now write up your age in figures. Again, draw a question mark and try to elicit the question. Model and drill as before and then write it up. Try to ensure that students are not writing anything at this stage. They should be concentrating on the sound of the words and trying to produce them accurately – writing them down will only distract from this. Also, the effort required to hold a question in your mind is greater than that needed to write it down, so it is more likely that the form will 'stick' and become active.

Continue like this, supplying bits of information about yourself and eliciting the question. As you go along, you can start to judge how much English the students have, and then tailor the difficulty of your prompts accordingly. If they seem quite good, try them with something that requires use of the past, or future. Here are some prompts you might use:

Toronto	*(Where are you from?)*
Canadian	*(What nationality are you?)*
678 9986	*(What's your telephone number?)*
Via Roma 18	*(What's your address?)*
Teacher	*(What do you do?)*
No, I'm single	*(Are you married?)*
Photography, reading	*(What do you do in your free time?)*
Marlboro	*(What cigarettes do you smoke?)*
Spain	*(Where did you go on holiday?)*
Sampdoria	*(Who will win the league championship?)*

When you have eight or nine questions on the board go back over them, checking pronunciation. Then rub the questions off the board and get the students to work in pairs writing them down. This should provide ample opportunity for you to wander round helping, correcting and generally playing the 'teacher'.

Next, draw on the board a table similar to the one shown below and get students to copy it (or give out prepared photocopies).

Name	Age	Address	Job	etc
Antonio				
Sergio				
Bianca				
etc				

Now students walk round chatting to each other filling in the table with all the information which they have just learned how to ask for.

As a final writing stage, everyone could choose one person they have interviewed and write up the information in a paragraph, adding any personal impressions they have of that person.

Another idea which is useful for helping people to get to know each other is to use a worksheet like the one below:

Name
Job
Married?
Favourite type of music
Favourite colour for clothes
Hobbies
Reason for learning English
Ideal man/woman
Ideal place for a holiday
Star sign
Idea of a perfect day

Get each student to sit opposite another student and look carefully at that person, imagining how they would complete the form. Students write down their suppositions and when they have finished, show them to the other person and discuss how close or far they were from the truth. This exercise does require a little imagination, but Italians usually have plenty of ideas and are very keen to discuss afterwards the truth or otherwise of their partner's impressions. When this stage is over, students can talk to someone else and tell them what they have discovered about their original partner. (Obviously this is only possible with students who already have some English.)

Some dos and don'ts for first lessons:

- Do prepare well, and look as if you know what you are doing.
- Do use tried and tested activities. This is no time for experiments.
- Do smile every now and then.
- Do try to get people's names sorted out as soon as possible.
- Do try to work out who your strong and weak students are.
- Don't single out students to speak in front of the whole class until they have had some time to settle down, and you are sure they will not be embarrassed.
- Don't expect people to know grammatical terms, especially at lower levels.
- Don't speak in Italian unless it is absolutely necessary.
- Don't try to start an activity until you are sure everybody knows what they have to do.
- Don't worry if things seem quiet – they will soon liven up.

CORRECTION

In general, Italians are not afraid of correction in the way, for example, Japanese students tend to be. They will not take it as personal criticism and they may even ask you to correct more than you want to. Nevertheless, no one likes to be made to look a fool, so even with Italians it is advisable to be sensitive.

When to correct. It is neither possible nor desirable to correct every mistake a student makes. When you are presenting or practising something, the focus is obviously on accuracy, and you should be strict. Correct thoroughly and immediately. When you are engaged in a communicative type activity, where fluency is the object, you can afford to be much more lenient, and correction can be at a later stage.

What to correct. In general, so as not to frighten people into silence, correct only what is directly relevant to the lesson or what is so inaccurate that it verges on incomprehensible. Remember also that it is pointless correcting mistakes which are to do with language areas not yet covered. Too much correction disheartens and inhibits, so decide what is important and leave it at that.

How to correct. The first step is to indicate that there is a mistake. You can do this by echoing what the student just said, getting him or her to repeat it or simply by looking quizzical. At this point the student will automatically run over what he or she has just said and try to find the problem. If this fails, you can help by indicating which word it is, or the type of mistake (verb? preposition?). If the student is still at a loss, ask if anyone else can 'help'. If no one can, you will have to explain, but it is usually better if correction comes from a source other than the teacher: it encourages people to be more aware of mistakes and to help each other.

THE FOUR SKILLS

Language teachers often talk about the 'four skills' – reading, writing, listening and speaking. Obviously there is more to teaching (and learning) a language than this. Each of these skills is made up of many other minor skills, and students need a knowledge of grammar, vocabulary and pronunciation to be able to function adequately in English.

Speaking and writing are called 'productive' skills, while listening and reading are 'receptive'.

	PRODUCTIVE	RECEPTIVE
ORAL	Speaking	Listening
WRITTEN	Writing	Reading

While you will already be using and practising one or more of these skills in the presentation and practice of new language, sometimes it is important to do activities whose prior purpose is to practise the skills themselves.

This section sets out a few ideas on ways to practise each of the four skills.

Listening

First of all it should be noted that 'doing listening' does not only mean listening to a cassette. It can also involve listening to the teacher, or a guest speaker, or other students – all of these are valid methods of practising the ability to understand the spoken word. For the sake of variety it is a good idea to remember and exploit them, and not become too dependent on the tape-recorder. However, as 'doing listening' from cassettes is both tricky and nearly always expected, I shall concentrate mostly on this.

A listening exercise with a cassette

In real life when people listen, it is usually because they are interested or they need to know something. You should remember this when practising the listening skill with students. If they do not have a reason to listen, they will take in very little. In some way you have to make students need or want to listen. This is in fact the prime purpose of the lead-in stage. By discussion or otherwise you try to arouse interest in the subject. Depending on the students and the subject matter of your listening material, this ranges from being quite simple to virtually impossible.

The (standard) progression of a listening exercise in class looks something like this:

(1) Lead-in.
(2) Teacher explains task.
(3) Students listen.
(4) Students compare in pairs or groups.
(5) Teacher gets answers from students.

Quite often, the third and fourth phases are considerably longer than this indicates. For example, many teachers get students to check with each other after one listening and then play the tape again, possibly holding another student-to-student checking session before going over the answers as a class. The advantages of this method are basically twofold: the checking in pairs not only practises speaking, but also shares out knowledge and raises questions, so that during the second listening students already have a good idea of the general sense of the passage and concentrate on listening for things they missed or that they were not sure about before.

Two or three times is usually enough for one tape. After this the amount of new information which students get becomes minimal, and the experience can be frustrating.

When answers have been given it is often possible to exploit the exercise further by getting students to do an activity related to the listening. For example, if the subject of the listening was a conversation in a shop, you could get pairs to prepare and perform similar conversations in a different type of shop.

Types of task to set. Tasks for listening exercises tend to be a straightforward series of questions about the content – sometimes the 'true or false' type, sometimes open ones. Remember, though, that there are alternatives. Students can have tables to fill in, diagrams to complete, or pictures to draw. Remember also that it is usually better to give students different tasks one at a time, and not to expect them to understand and recall everything at once. In this way you can ease students into the text stage by stage, starting with the gist, moving on to more detailed comprehension and then perhaps focusing on the type of language used.

This gradual approach is especially suited to Italian students, as they are often impatient and want to understand everything straight away. By giving them a simple gist task first, which they can get 90% or 100% right, you give their confidence a good boost and distract them from the (for them) worrying fact that they may have understood only 30% of the text as a whole. Then they can listen again for details which escaped them the first time.

Imagine you are working with a tape of two shoppers buying things in a grocer's. The stages of listening might look like this:

TYPE OF TASK	EXAMPLE QUESTIONS
'Gist'	**How many people are there?** **What is their relationship?** **Where are they?**
More detailed comprehension	**What drinks do they buy?** **How many eggs does the woman want?** **How much are the cakes?**
Language focus	**How does the woman ask for the eggs?** **('Give me 6 eggs, will you')**

Speaking

Just as students need a reason to listen, they need a reason to speak. While inevitably sometimes they will be speaking because the teacher has told them to, it is obviously better if there is some real communication going on – that is, if the speaker wants or needs to give certain information to somebody else. This desire or need to communicate is often called an 'information gap'.

To a certain extent all the examples of class speaking activities given in this section are based on the 'information gap' – even a free discussion involves giving opinions, and opinions are new 'information' for the listener. However, for the sake of clarity I have divided the activities into four groups: information gap;

personalization; role plays; and discussions. In the first, I have limited the examples to those in which the 'gap' is ostensibly created by the teacher.

Information gap

Tourists. This is one of the simplest examples of information gap activities. You have three or four students who represent the railway station, the bus station, the tourist office, etc. Each has information prepared by the teacher. The other students are tourists and they have a list of things they have to find out. For example:

> **Find out times, prices and other details about the following:**
> **the museum;**
> **trains to London;**
> **buses to the beach;**
> **a cheap hotel near the sea;**
> **cinema (what films?)**

Thus to complete the task the students have to visit all the different information points and ask for certain information.

Jigsaw story construction. In this activity, students are given part of a story which they have to complete by obtaining the rest from other students. You can do this with pictures as well as the written word. Find a simple story which can be divided into four or five parts, or expressed in four or five pictures and put students into groups of that number. Give out the information, get students to memorize it (you could even take it back from them to ensure they do not show it to anyone). Then groups discuss what they know until they manage to reconstruct the story.

Explaining how to do something. The principle is simply this – you show half your students how to make an origami frog, or build something in Lego, or tie a complicated knot and they have to teach someone how to do it. It works best if the task students are set has a tangible, and therefore very satisfying end result. Underline that 'teachers' can speak only when they are explaining; they must not touch anything – otherwise they do not have to work so hard at finding the right words and expressing themselves clearly.

Personalization

There is nothing people like talking about so much as themselves, and Italians are no exception to this. If you can get them to relate language to themselves and their personal existence, you have gone a long way towards helping them acquire it. Here are two of the most obvious ways of using this principle.

Student talks. Whatever language you have been teaching, it is always possible to relate it somehow to students' own lives. From this it is a short step to getting them to tell other students about it. Imagine you have been looking at future forms. Each student will have some idea of what is going to happen to them over the next year, and it will probably be quite close to their hearts. Give them a little time to think and prepare, and then they can talk about it for as long as they want and are able. If the class is small, students could address the whole class. If numbers are larger, or students are too self-conscious, it can be done in closed pairs. In either case encourage other students to ask questions.

Questionnaires. A good way to encourage students to talk about themselves is by using questionnaires. These have the advantage that they can be built around teaching points like a vocabulary area or a point of grammar. Alternatively, they can have a theme, like films, music, or anything of interest to the students. Generally they work best with students working in pairs, asking each other the questions and expanding on the responses as and when they want. To round off the exercise you can do a feedback session with the whole class. Go through the questions getting students to tell the others about anything interesting or surprising they have discovered.

Role plays

Role plays try to give a semblance of reality to the practising of English in the classroom. The teacher asks students to imagine they are in a 'real-life' situation (a restaurant, a traffic accident, a business meeting, etc) and to speak and react as they would in that situation. The aim is to give students the experience of using English as a living language, rather than as an artificial classroom activity.

Embarrassing as the idea may seem, given enough preparation and encouragement, most Italians throw themselves into role plays with very satisfying enthusiasm. Depending on the level and inventiveness of your students, they can have roles which are completely defined by you, or they can invent their role as they go along.

It is important to give students some form of feedback when the role play is over. A good method is to make notes of what is said during the activity, concentrating not only on the mistakes and unsatisfactory English, but also on examples of English used well and correctly.

Here are two examples of role plays you might try.

Art gallery. Some work on the vocabulary of art may be useful as a preparation for this activity, as well as pictures of paintings, sculptures, etc. Students are directors of an art gallery which has a sum of money to spend on new works of art. They have to pretend that they are at the directors' meeting which decides what works to buy. The teacher can assign them roles – for example: 'You are Fred Davis. You are a 56-year-old company director with a strong interest in classical sculpture. You think the gallery should extend its collection in this direction. You hate every aspect of 20th century painting.'

Alternatively, students can follow their own feelings and preferences about the art which is for sale.

Make sure that the sum of money the directors have available is enough to buy only about half of the things you show them. In this way a lively debate is almost inevitable.

Restaurant. This role play is a natural extension to any work about food, or the function of asking for things. Divide students into 'waiters' and 'customers'. Again, you can either let them be themselves in the situation, or give them characters (a deaf waiter, a young business man trying to impress a first date, an irritable pensioner who complains about the price of everything, etc). One of the keys to the success of this role play work lies in the 'props'. Try to get photocopies of menus to consult, a few wine bottles, music in the background, pads and pencils for the waiters, and move the furniture around so that the room looks more like a restaurant. All this contributes to increasing expectations and raising the fun, play-acting element.

Discussions

Discussions are probably the least artificial of the speaking activities which you can do with groups of students. They involve genuine communication and a minimum of teacher interference. Unfortunately, however, they are highly unpredictable. Sometimes they can get started very quickly and be satisfying for everybody, and sometimes they fail completely to arouse any interest and fall flat even before anyone has said anything. So if you plan to a have a discussion in a class, have a reserve activity ready in case it does not take off.

You can structure discussions in a number of ways. Here are two of the most common.

Order of importance. With this method students are given a list of things to put in order (see the example in the box below). Students work alone initially and then discuss in small groups, each trying to convince the others of his or her order. The exercise is over when each group has agreed on an order.

This method can be used with almost any subject matter, and one of its positive points is that it starts with something concrete to work from (a list), and so does not get lost in abstractions.

Two sides of the argument. Choose your topic, for example 'capital punishment', and divide the class into two groups: those in favour and those against. The groups then try to think of as many arguments as they can to support their point of view. When you think they are ready, invite one side to advance an argument and encourage the other to counter it. With luck this should start off a discussion.

With large classes it may be better to organize a discussion in groups as some people will be intimidated by speaking in front of a lot of people.

INVENTIONS MOST USEFUL TO MANKIND

The wheel	**The internal**	**Printing press**
The computer	**combustion engine**	**Penicillin**
Nuclear energy	**Fire**	**The telephone**
Artificial insemination	**Gunpowder**	**Plastic**

Some things Italians like talking about:

- Mafia and corruption.
- Love and relationships.
- The Italian national character – does it exist?
- Differences between northerners and southerners.
- The Italian education system (compared to the system in your country).
- The usefulness (or otherwise) of cellular telephones.
- Life after death and the supernatural.
- Food.

Reading

Much of what is said above about listening is also valid for reading. Just as with a tape it is best to take comprehension in stages – a written text can be read several times for different purposes, and for differing degrees of detail.

How students read and why they need practice

The problem with reading is that, unlike a tape which goes at its own speed, a written text can be read at any speed. Italians, like students anywhere, have a tendency to want to understand everything, even though this is a highly unrealistic aim for most. When they read, they pay too much attention to what they do not understand and insufficient attention to what they do, with the result that they read slowly and ponderously, stopping frequently to ask a meaning or look up a word.

It is difficult, but important, to persuade students that they can do most reading exercises perfectly well without understanding many parts of the text. You can point out that if students ever go to London, for example, there will be many times when they will not understand everything, but this does not mean they should give up and go home! If they have the ability to home in quickly on the information they need, and ignore those parts of the text which they cannot understand they will read the language with more confidence. A key challenge for the teacher, then, is getting them to concentrate on the task, and do what they can with what they understand.

Types of task

There are several different types of task you can set students to do while reading, and they correspond more or less to the reasons why people generally read.

To extract specific information. When you want to see what is on TV at 10 pm you do not read the whole newspaper. You go to the TV page, and look at what is written near 10 pm. Similarly for students, give them a few quite detailed, but simple questions about a text which is long and dispersive. This will help train them to locate what they need quickly.

For 'gist'. For this type of exercise it is vital that students have a time limit and that the questions are not about irrelevant details, but the central points of the text.

For detailed comprehension. There are occasions when it is normal to read with a need to understand everything – instructions for a new electronic toy, for example. These texts are never very long, however, and so if you want students to do this type of close reading make sure you choose a fairly short piece. Make your questions precise and relevant.

To learn new language. This is clearly something which non-native speakers do more than natives (although they do it too). A reading text can be used to focus attention on new language, as well as simply to practise comprehension. Questions which do this help train the reader to look analytically at texts and use them as a source of information about the language. Some examples of 'language focus' questions are:

- How does the writer begin the story?
- How many times does the verb 'look' appear? Is it always followed by the same preposition? Does it always have exactly the same meaning?
- Which word in the third sentence suggests a contrast with the second sentence?
- What does 'it' refer to in the first line?

Writing

The value of writing

Many Italians, once they have finished their education, write very little, even in their own language. The only time they put pen to paper is to write a shopping list or a brief message to a friend or work colleague. For this reason you might decide that teaching 'writing' in English is a waste of time.

On the other hand, it is undoubtedly true that putting language down in a fixed form does help students fix it in their minds and clarify their notions of how it works. So at least as a way of reinforcing and practising new language, its value is assured.

Getting people to write

While most Italian students are quite happy to produce short isolated phrases as part of an exercise, extended writing (essays, stories, etc) is a different story. Realistically speaking, many Italian students never write much more than those few practice sentences, or answers to questions which are absolutely necessary in the lesson. You can set as many compositions as you like for homework – some people just do not like writing, and there will always be a reason why they could not do it.

This does not mean that you should give up hope altogether. Many students do like writing and will do whatever task you set them. Keep setting writing homework, perhaps as an alternative to some exercises, and those students who want to take advantage will do so.

One way of encouraging slightly hesitant writers is to start up a correspondence between yourself and individual students. After the first lesson of the course, ask the class to write you a letter for their homework. They can talk about themselves, their interests, feelings about English, anything they want. Take the letters in, mark them, and write a brief note back. It does not have to be much – just enough to ask a few questions and imply that you expect an answer. Some students will carry on the correspondence, others will drop it immediately. The important thing is that there is a channel for students who want to write to use whenever they want.

This idea appeals to many Italian students because they feel that (a) they are getting some individual attention; and (b) as a result they are establishing a more personal relationship.

VOCABULARY

Lack of vocabulary is one of the biggest barriers to fluency, and naturally it is something which worries Italian students of English. There are two things you can do to help them expand their word-power: first, ensure that all students have a notebook for new words and that they use it; second, encourage students to read as much as possible outside the lessons. This is the most painless way of absorbing words and their meanings.

When new words come up in the course of a lesson, there are several ways in which you can convey the meaning. Obviously you will choose whichever way is possible and seems most efficient in the circumstances.

Pictures. These can be drawn by you on the board or brought in to the class in the form of flash-cards or cut-outs from magazines. One book which can help you develop your skill at drawing recognizable pictures is *1000 Pictures for Teachers to Copy* by Andrew Wright (Collins).

Realia. In other words, the objects themselves. Clearly this is great for small, tangible things like 'pen' or 'wallet', but is not much good for abstract concepts like 'imagination'.

Mime. This method is useful and effective for many verbs like 'run' or 'fall', and can also be used for most prepositions.

Opposites. You can sometimes get meanings over by telling students what the opposite is. Thus 'open' can be explained by contrast with 'closed'. Of course it only works if students understand the opposite. ('Opposite' in Italian is *contrario*).

At the beginning of an elementary course I was doing, the word 'bang' came up and I started to explain what it meant. I said it was a 'big noise', but that only confused them because it sounded like *noia* in Italian which means 'boredom'. Seeing that I was getting nowhere I thumped the board hoping to get some sort of noise out of it. It must have been loose because it immediately fell to the floor with a huge 'crash', if not quite a 'bang'. Evidently the word stuck because by the end of the course I was still seeing the word 'bang' crop up regularly in students' compositions. Most of the other words I had taught 'without mishap' had soon been forgotten, but this one remained because it was mentally linked to a particular occasion.

Mark Readman (Australia)

Examples. Words that signify a class or category of things can be explained by listing some examples. 'Fruit', for instance, is easily understood as soon as you start talking about apples, oranges and bananas.

Explanation. Sometimes a brief verbal explanation can get meaning across, especially if students are at a level at which they can follow your words without difficulty. You have to be careful, however, not to confuse matters further by introducing more words that they do not understand.

Translation. Viewed by many as bad practice, it does however offer a simple solution when nothing else seems to be working. Clearly it is counter-productive if it happens all the time, because students are less likely to remember knowledge which comes too easily. Getting students to look a word up does at least make them active in the process, although it can be too distracting and time-consuming to be worthwhile.

PRONUNCIATION

Correct pronunciation is the sum of factors too numerous to mention. However, for the sake of teaching they can be divided into:

- Sounds;
- Stress;
- Intonation;
- Linking and elision.

All of these elements contribute to the differences between the speech of a native speaker and that of an Italian. Opinions vary as to how important this difference is, and in the early stages of learning there is a strong case for correcting pronunciation only when it interferes with understanding. Later on students might want to eliminate the aspects of their pronunciation which are most glaringly 'Italian', but there is no reason why intelligible Italian English should not sit alongside Glaswegian or New York English as perfectly acceptable variations on a theme.

When doing pronunciation work in class, on any of the areas discussed here, there a few things you should remember:

(1) Make it snappy – labouring a point already grasped will not help.
(2) Don't demand perfection – it is not necessary and you will rarely get it.
(3) Be wary of giving the pronunciation of isolated words; they can sound quite different in the middle of a phrase.
(4) Ultimately you are the model, have faith in what you think sounds right.

Sounds

Italians have problems with the English sound system, especially the vowel sounds, because in Italian every letter is pronounced, and always in the same way. 'A' is always as in 'cat', 'E' as in 'bed', 'I' as in 'did', 'O' as in 'hot' and 'U' as in 'put'. In English there are at least twenty vowel sounds and often there seems to be little governing logic.

The following are some of the things you can do to help students get sounds right.

Model the correct pronunciation and get students to repeat. This is the most obvious, simplest, and arguably most effective way to teach pronunciation.

Use a phonemic chart. The phonemic alphabet was invented specifically to help people produce precise sounds. If you feel at home with it, it can be very useful for pinpointing differences. For example 'Tuesday' and 'Thursday' often sound very similar when said by Italian learners and the difference can be very precisely demonstrated by representing them as /tju:zdeɪ/ and /θɜ:zdeɪ/.

Use 'minimal pairs'. This means demonstrating sound by contrasting it with a similar one in a series of word pairs. For example:

   grin   green

fill   **feel**
still   **steal**
hit   **heat**

Italians generally have difficulty distinguishing between the vowel sounds represented in these two columns (/I/ and /iː/). By listening to you saying them, however, they should start to hear a difference and with a little practice they will pronounce them more precisely. A good test is to get individuals to say one of the words at random, while you point to the one you understand. Afterwards you can indicate the spelling patterns which produce these two sounds.

Draw attention to the position of your mouth, teeth and tongue. Students will sometimes be able to reproduce sounds better if they watch you. An obvious example is the 'th' sound, which Italians rarely use. By pointing to your tongue sticking out between your teeth, you may help them make the right noise. It has to be said, however, that this method is more often amusing than useful.

For more information on the particular sounds which Italians find difficult, see the section on 'Pronunciation' in Chapter 12.

Stress

'Stress' refers to where the emphasis is put in a word or phrase. 'Italian', for example, is pronounced with the stress on the second syllable, not the first or third. Ways of marking it include:

Italian
It'alian
It<u>a</u>lian
Italian (○ ◯ ○)
It-AL-ian

In the fourth example the larger circle represents the stress. As with most aspects of pronunciation, the most straightforward way of helping students is simply to get them to repeat it after you. Some other ideas which might be useful are:

- Try to remember to mark the stress when putting new vocabulary on the board.
- Draw students' attention to the way it is shown in dictionaries (usually as in the second example above).
- Every now and then do exercises in which students put words into groups according to the stress pattern.
- Put up pieces of paper round the class with the most common stress patterns marked at the top (◯○○, ○◯○, ○○◯, etc). Then, when new words come up, students can write them on the

appropriate chart, gradually building a list for each one. After a time you will have only to point at one of the charts for students to know where the stress goes on a word.

Sentence stress

Stress is also important in complete sentences, where it is placed on the most important words (usually verbs and nouns):

He <u>went</u> to <u>Milan</u> to <u>see</u> her <u>face</u>.

In this respect Italian is similar to English, so it should not create too many problems. Nevertheless, occasionally clapping out the rhythm of sentences helps to make students more aware of natural speech rhythms and how they bring language alive. Limericks and nursery rhymes are another, fun way to get classes to work on stress. Italians generally appreciate this type of activity, especially if you present it as a game.

Weak and strong

The notion of weak and strong pronunciation is connected to the question of stress, and it is worth pointing out to Italians because in their own language there is no such concept. For this reason it can be very difficult to convince people that the correct pronunciation of 'He went to the station', is not the same as the sounds of each individual word strung together. In fact, 'to' and 'the' are pronounced weakly. The vowel sound that we put after 't' and 'th' is called a *schwa* /ə/ and it is very common in English. It always occurs on a word or part of a word which is not stressed (this is not to say that every unstressed vowel is a schwa).

Compare the pronunciation of these words on their own and in phrases.

> *at*   **he lives at the end**
> *of*   **ten of spades**
> *for* **we had chicken for dinner**

It is easy for students to come away with the idea that this type of pronunciation is not 'good' English – that it is somehow lazy – and it is important to make it clear that it is not. When Italians talk about how English speakers do not talk properly, swallowing words and failing to enunciate ('*mangiano le parole*') what they are referring to is the fact that they cannot hear the words which are not stressed and therefore not pronounced in the strong form they recognize.

A good way to get people to produce the schwa is to write 'U' on the board and get them to say it. They will give you a sound which is too strong. Tell them to say it as if they were very tired, and had no energy. This time the result should be something resembling a schwa. Then get them to put the same sound in the middle of 'Italy'.

To make students sensitive to the use of weak and strong forms, a good exercise is for you to say naturally some sentences which they have written down, and for them to mark first the stress, and secondly where the schwa appears.

Intonation

Intonation (the changes of pitch and volume in speech) is difficult to teach formally because it is largely unconscious, and, as soon as you try to focus on it, it can sound false and even ridiculous.

Nevertheless, students need to be aware that intonation conveys a lot of information about the feelings and interest of the speaker. The dialogue below can be used to illustrate this point:

(*In a train*)
A: Hello.
B: Hello.
A: Where are you going?
B: Florence. And you?
A: Bologna. I'm going to see a friend.
B: Really!
A: What are you going for?
B: I've got a job interview.
A: Oh! That's good.
B: Yes.

Ask a student to take part **A**, and you take **B**. When you respond, put as much friendly energy into the answers as possible. Then ask how interested and friendly **B** seemed. Then repeat the dialogue but this time **B** responds with a flat, bored intonation. Ask students to tell you the difference between the two versions, and finally practise in pairs.

Linking and elision

'Linking' is the term used to describe how there are usually no pauses between words in spoken English. This is partly a question of how quickly you speak, and practice will help. However, the way 'job interview' becomes 'jo binterview' will seem curious to Italians, because in Italian words always finish with vowels and so they flow on from each other without any help.

As with other aspects of pronunciation, this is best handled by students repeating the teacher's model. To give it more explicit attention, you can get students to draw a sign between linked words in a text (see below) and then read it accordingly.

Damien ͜ opened his ͜ eyes ͜ and saw his ͜ aunt . . .

'Elision' happens when parts of words go missing in spoken English. 'Do not', for example, becomes 'don't'. This particular example is not much of a problem, but Italians can get quite exasperated when they see 'will not' become 'won't' or 'I would' become 'I'd'.

Their dislike of these contracted forms is partly due to the fact that in Italian such things are generally confined to dialects, and so are not considered 'proper' Italian. Conversely, in English it is absolutely acceptable to pronounce 'I'm going to kill him' as 'I'm gonna kill 'im'.

Because most of the contractions involve verb forms in the various tenses, it is a good idea to present them when you present the tenses. In this way students are aware of the form 'I'd' and 'won't' from the moment they become acquainted with the tense itself. Some common contractions are:

not	**n't**
is	**'s**
has	**'s**
had	**'d**
would	**'d**
will	**'ll**
will not	**won't**
going to	**gonna**
want to	**wanna**

VIDEO

There are many good reasons for using video in the classroom: students generally react enthusiastically to the idea; they see people engaged in realistic dialogue; they can follow the story even without understanding much dialogue; and it commands attention in a way that a tape recorder cannot.

On the other hand, it does have its drawbacks. Apart from any embarrassing problems you may have operating the machine, the most serious disadvantage is connected to the initially positive feeling which students have towards video. When they see a video recorder, they are happy because they expect to be entertained, and so they settle back into a passive viewing mode. Then they find you are 'ruining' their enjoyment by stopping, starting, asking questions and giving out exercises. To avoid disgruntlement for this reason, whenever possible let students watch the whole scene at least once without interruption. It is very advisable to give them a simple task to do, but for the first viewing it should be light and not too distracting. Two or three 'gist' questions are quite enough.

There are several textbooks available which are apparently full of ideas for using video. In fact, they contain a handful of basic ideas reworked in a myriad of different variations. The basic strategies are these:

- Watch and answer questions (comprehension).
- Watch without sound and predict dialogue.
- Listen to soundtrack and predict situation.
- Watch and give running commentary.
- Act out a section of video.

Watch and answer questions

This is the simplest way of using video and is really no more than the comprehension tasks used for reading and listening transferred to a different format. A few things to bear in mind:

(1) Make sure some of your questions are about visual information so that weaker students can do something even if they do not understand much of what is said.

(2) Use your questions to help students understand what is happening by focusing attention on the important elements of the action and the dialogue. For example, if a phrase is important but difficult to understand, write it out and ask who says it.

(3) When choosing a piece of video, pay particular attention to the sound quality and the amount of background noise. It is unrealistic to expect students to cope with the same levels you can tolerate. If you turn the screen away from you, you will get a much better idea of how 'comprehensible' the soundtrack will be.

(4) Also make sure that the section you choose is not too long. Students will probably stand a video longer than an audio-cassette, but they tire of it too. Ten minutes of sustained dialogue is already stretching it for anything except advanced classes.

(5) Make sure that students do not have to write very much down while they are viewing. It is easy for them to miss important visual information if they have to write and they may not get the overall understanding they need. Save any writing for later, when they are not trying to do two things at once.

If you can build an information gap into the comprehension exercises, then you have the basis for some speaking practice too.

Select a sequence containing a fair amount of action and a visible story-line, and divide the class into two groups. Show one group the first half and the other the second half of the video. If you give out question sheets to each group, these will help them understand and recall what they see. When both groups have seen their section and answered the questions, ask them to form pairs with one member from each group, and tell each other what they saw. Finally, they can reconstruct the complete story by putting prepared prompts in order.

Watch without sound and predict dialogue

Watching without the sound, people still receive a great deal of information about characters, the situation and the substance of the dialogue. It is an excellent lead-in to detailed comprehension work, because it tunes students into the situation and encourages them to imagine what sort of language would be produced in this context. In fact, soundless video provides perfect visual cues for students to construct their own dialogues.

Having produced a suitable script, they can watch again with sound and compare their version to the original. Give praise to people who have produced a feasible dialogue, even if it differs substantially from what is on the video.

Taking this idea a step further, the whole class can come to an agreed version and then try to match it exactly to the 'talking heads' on the video, so that the speech corresponds to the gestures and length of time the characters keep opening their mouths.

In the end, students can take roles and speak 'for' the characters on video. For this type of exercise it is not even necessary to hear the original version.

Listen with no picture

Unless you are careful, this can end up being just a dreadfully difficult listening exercise, so be very selective about what you use. It should:

- be fairly lively;
- contain comprehensible speech;
- have at least two characters;
- include lots of other sounds and noises; and
- take no longer than a listening exercise on cassette.

Judging by the content of the dialogue, the voices and the other noises, it should be possible to acquire a fairly clear picture of what is going on.

Get students in groups to compare their ideas about 'who',

'where' and 'why', and to build up a comprehensive scenario. They should also imagine what gestures and movements accompany the speech.

When they have imagined all they can, you can show them the video with the picture, at which point students should be very motivated to see how their ideas correspond to the original. Also, while concentrating on the visual aspect, they will be absorbing the speech which is reflected in the actions and movements on the screen.

A variation, which stimulates discussion, is to position half the class so they can see the screen, and the other half so they can only hear. After viewing, the non-viewing half find a partner from the other half and explain what they understood of the action and what they imagine about the scene. The viewing partners can then fill them in on the details of what they saw and how accurate their partners have been.

Watch and give a running commentary

This is an excellent strategy for promoting fluency. At its most straightforward, it consists of individuals, or everyone at once, shouting out what is happening. At low levels this will probably just comprise isolated nouns, verbs and possibly adjectives, but this exercise can be valid in itself as a way of flushing out the pipes between perception and expression. Speeding up this process of commenting on the action is one of the key factors in improving speaking skills.

If you want to give more structure to the exercise, divide the class into two and put them on different sides of the room. Then, with one side viewing, they can take it in turns to give a commentary of what they see. If you can find a ball, or some similar object, give it to the first student who holds it for as long as he or she talks. When the student cannot or does not want to continue, he or she gives the ball to the next person who takes over the responsibility of commentating.

While this is happening the other students should be trying to visualize what is being described. When the section of video is finished, the other group has a go (with the same section) and the first group visualizes (and remembers) the images of the action. The second team should pick up on the language used by the first group, and build on it.

When both sides have done it once, you can step in and point out some useful vocabulary or any unsatisfactory language which was used. If there is enough interest, ask both teams to do it again, still with the same piece of video. This time both teams should be more fluent and, hopefully, more accurate.

Acting out a section of video

Any form of acting usually goes down well with Italians, and from a linguistic viewpoint it is useful because, by assigning words and phrases to individual students, the language starts to become their personal property.

The piece of video you choose should not be more than two or three minutes long and it should contain at least two characters engaged in action as well as simply talking.

There are several ways to approach this idea, and the viewing of the video can come before, during or after the acting. Here are three possibilities:

(1) Give out copies of the script on which the names of the speakers have been removed (it should not even show how many people are speaking). In groups students study the script and try to deduce how many people are involved in the sequence and who says what. To do this they will have to have a very clear understanding of the text and this will be important for what comes next. Get them also to think about the situation where the dialogue takes place and the emotions of the people involved. Having done this, ask students to take a role each (according to however many they have decided are necessary) and act out the piece, standing up, walking round or doing whatever seems appropriate to the text. Finally, show the original video and invite discussion about the differences between it and the class interpretations. Students will be very interested when they watch the video because they will identify personally with at least one character. What is more they should have little trouble understanding the flow of speech, because by now they know it inside out. For this reason this exercise can be a powerful boost to confidence.

(2) For this you will need a section of video in which the speech is not continuous, but limited to frequent short phrases. Show the video once for general comprehension and then get each student to choose one character and to 'mirror', that is copy, every move that character makes as you all watch a second time. Then watch a third time with students repeating out loud whatever their character says (or whatever they understand of it). Finally, you might try to repeat the whole thing without the video. It will get a lot of laughs even if not entirely successful.

(3) In this activity you can leave all the work to the students. You simply show them a short segment, write up the number on the tape counter at the start and finish, and leave the room, saying that you will return in about ten or fifteen minutes. In the

meantime they can review the section as much as they want, write it out, remember it, whatever they want, but when you return they must be ready to act it out as fully as possible. After the initial panic, students usually manage to organize themselves enough to produce something similar to the video. You will have to give them longer than fifteen minutes, however. The time limit serves only to galvanize them into action, and if you listen outside the door you should get a good idea of when the right moment arrives to make your re-entry.

SONGS

Many Italians have at home records by Pink Floyd, Dire Straits, U2, to name only the most common. This means that many are open to English in music in a way in which few are to English in their course book or other 'scholastic' materials. This fact alone makes it a crime not to use songs, at least occasionally. Here are some more good reasons:

- They are absolutely authentic.
- They are memorable.
- They are enjoyable.
- There is a huge variety of subject matter.
- It does not have to be the teacher who chooses them.

In general try to select songs which you can at least understand without too much difficulty and which are in a style which is unlikely to alienate anybody – punk rock, for instance, will go against the grain for many Italians, who are used to more melodic, less aggressive popular music.

Italians usually appreciate old songs which have become classics, and therefore familiar, and recent songs which they will have heard on the radio, TV or in clubs. Here is a list (by no means comprehensive) of what young Italians will be familiar with and will therefore be all the happier to study in class:

- The Beatles (and John Lennon).
- The Doors.
- Elton John.
- George Michael.
- Madonna.
- Marvin Gaye.
- Queen.
- Sting (and some Police).
- U2.

As well as simply listening to a song, there are several exercises you can do to involve students more actively.

Gap-fill. This involves giving out a copy of the song lyrics on which some words have been blanked out. Students listen and fill in the blanks. Instead of just making the gaps random, you can blank out the adjectives, pronouns, verbs in the past tense, or anything which crops up frequently and which you want to practise.

Bingo. There are a few variations of this. One is to write on the board (or dictate) about twelve words, half of which occur in the song. Students then listen and tick the ones they hear. Alternatively, put up a list of words from the song and ask students to choose eight or nine. Then, as they listen, they cross off each of their words as it comes up. The first person to hear all their words is the winner.

Ordering. This also involves a list of words from the song, but this time they have to be put in the order in which they occur. This is a useful activity to do with a song that contains new vocabulary. Once you have presented the words, students, by trying to order them, have to recognize the pronunciation in a natural context.

Wrong words. Prepare a transcript of the song words, in which there are a few wrong words. Try to include words which are conceivable alternatives, or which sound similar so as not to make the exercise too easy. Then students listen and correct the 'mistakes'.

Jumbled words. Put the words of a few song lines in the wrong order. You might want to give students time before listening to decide what they think is the correct order, and then listen to check.

Jumbled lines. Prepare a transcript in which the lines of each verse (or even the whole song) are mixed up. Students then listen and put them in the right order. As with 'jumbled words' (above) you might want to give students time first to guess the right order. If you have time and a pair of scissors, you can cut up the transcript into individual lines which students then have to move physically into the correct position.

11 Teaching grammar and functions

This chapter provides an overview of grammatical structures and the uses to which they are put (functions), and discusses specific teaching ideas and techniques.

GRAMMAR

If you have already taught English, little of this section will be new to you. If you have not, I hope it will be useful for reference, first to clarify the grammatical concepts in your own mind and, second, to prepare you for possible problems and give you some ideas for your teaching.

There is of course more to English grammar than what you will find here – however, I have tried to cover all the standard structures and concepts which crop up again and again in any teaching situation. If you require further information concerning any point of grammar, consult one of the two by now classic English grammar books: Michael Swan's *Practical English Usage* (Oxford University Press) or the *Collins Cobuild English Grammar*.

In the sections which follow, an (*x*) after a sentence denotes incorrect or unnatural English.

Tenses

Teaching verb tenses forms the heart of many grammar syllabi, and what follows is a brief examination of each tense, designed to start you off rather than to be absolute and definitive.

Bear in mind when teaching beginners that some people may not be familiar with standard concepts such as 'first-person singular'. Although the same system is used in Italian (eg *prima persona singolare*), students who have not studied grammar before may be a little bewildered the first time you use such terms.

Likewise, always be ready to underline the fact that the six English tenses do not always correspond to the Italian tenses.

What is more, they often have more than one meaning. This is also true in Italian, but students probably will not be aware of it because few people think about their own language to the extent they think about one they are learning.

Present simple

Meaning. The present simple is used to describe habitual actions (**Tommaso gets up at 6 o'clock**), present states (**Francesca lives in Milan**) and general truths (**Rome is the capital of Italy**). It is also sometimes used for timetabled events in the future (**We arrive in Florence at 10.15**). This last usage is best ignored to start with as it will only confuse beginners.

Form. In the affirmative the basic verb stem is used. The only complication is the 's' which is added in the third person singular. The negative and the interrogative use the auxiliary 'do', or 'does' in the third person singular:

> **I eat.   I don't eat.   Do I eat?**
> **She eats.   She doesn't eat.   Does she eat?**

Teaching. The meaning of this tense poses few problems for Italians as it is very similar to their own present tense. The problems will be to do with producing the right form at the right time. Students frequently forget the third person 's' and often produce negatives and interrogatives without the auxiliary. This is because Italian has no auxiliary in the present. Thus mistakes like these are common:

> **I not go.   You go?   Go you?**   (*x*)

The mistakes in the question form are due to the way the Italian language makes interrogatives – ie either with intonation or by inverting subject and verb.

It may take students some time to get the hang of manipulating verbs and auxiliaries because the system is so different from Italian. However, it is worth spending time on this because, as learners advance, they will encounter the same system in all the other tenses, and if they understand how the present simple works, they should have fewer problems with the auxiliaries in other tenses.

Present continuous/progressive

Meaning. This tense is used to express an action happening at the time of speaking (**He's speaking to Manuela**), a temporary state

(**I'm living in Rome at the moment**), or a fixed arrangement for the future (**They're going to the beach tomorrow**). As with the present simple's future use, it is best to leave the last meaning till you deal with the future tense later on.

Form. It uses the verb 'to be' as the auxiliary, plus the present participle (verb stem plus 'ing'). Unlike the present simple, the auxiliary is present in the affirmative as well as the negative and interrogative. The negative adds 'not' or 'n't' to the auxiliary, while the interrogative inverts subject and auxiliary:

He is swimming.   He isn't swimming.   Is he swimming?

Teaching. The first time you teach this tense, it is important to get across the idea that the action is happening now. To practise it you can use pictures of people doing things, or better still a video sequence where it is obvious that the action is now and it is natural to use the continuous. Another idea is to blindfold students and get the others to perform various actions noisily, so that the blindfolded students can guess what they are doing.

Problems. Italian has a similar tense formed in a similar way ('stare' + present participle), so neither the meaning nor the form should be particularly problematic. Sometimes students get hold of the idea that '. . . ing' is important, but forget to use the auxiliary 'to be'. As before, they often forget to invert subject and auxiliary in the question form. Thus mistakes like **I coming** and **You are going?** are common.

Students will probably not use the contracted forms of 'to be'. Try to get them to say 'I'm', 'you're', etc instead of the awkward 'I am walking', with too much stress on the 'to be' auxiliary.

There are some verbs in English which are never used in the continuous. They are called 'stative' verbs and, as the name suggests, refer to verbs describing a state ('be', 'know', 'like', 'love', 'have' in the sense of 'possess', etc). You may want to deal with these at a later date, when the mechanics of the continuous form have been mastered.

Simple past

Meaning. The simple past describes a completed action at a known point in the past or within a fixed frame of reference, as in a narrative (**We visited Venice last weekend**).

Form. Here students are introduced to the idea of regular and irregular verbs. Regular verbs add 'ed' to the verb stem while irregular verbs have forms, often quite different, which must be learnt.

> look – **looked**
> work – **worked**
> go – **went**
> see – **saw**

The negative and interrogative forms work just like the present simple, except that the auxiliary is 'did', not 'do':

> **I don't look / Do I look? – I didn't look / Did I look?**
> **We don't go / Do we go? – We didn't go / Did we go?**

Teaching. Picture stories are a good way of introducing and practising the simple past. Alternatively, you can focus on the students' own lives and get them to talk about the important events in their lives so far, or about their last summer holiday. This last option lends itself particularly well to practising the question form , as students can interview each other about where they went, who they went with, what they did, etc.

Depending on how important you feel pronunciation is, you might like to teach the three different pronunciations of the 'ed' ending. It depends on the pronunciation of the last sound in the verb (eg 't' as in 'kissed'; 'd' as in 'tamed', 'id' as in batted').

Problems. Generally, this tense is not too difficult for students to comprehend. They will not perceive any problems in its usage until they encounter the present perfect (see below).

Things to watch out for are, as ever, mistakes in the formation of negatives and questions. As well as the usual tendency to ignore the auxiliary, students often use the past form where it is not required, as in:

> **He didn't went.**   (*x*)
> **Did you saw her?**   (*x*)

Point out that in negatives and interrogatives it is the 'did' which indicates the past; the verb itself stays in its base form. Confusion may arise when students translate past tenses from Italian. All three past tenses in Italian can sometimes be translated with the English simple past:

> *(passato prossimo) Sono andato a Firenze.* – **I went to Florence.**
> *(passato remoto) Andai a Firenze.* – **I went to Florence.**
> *(imperfetto) Andavo a Firenze ogni finesettimana.* – **I went to Florence every weekend.**

You can point this out to students so that they do not feel they are necessarily making a mistake by always using the simple past.

Of course, there are times when the simple past will not be correct but you cannot penalize students for not using a tense which you have not presented, so wait until they have seen all the English past tenses before getting fussy over translations.

Past continuous

Meaning. Generally this is used either to set the scene in a narrative (**The wind was howling, snow was falling**) or to describe an action in progress at a specific time in the past (**I was watching TV when the bomb went off**).

Form. The form is 'was/were' plus present participle (. . . 'ing' form). It may be useful to show students that the form is the same as the present continuous except that the auxiliary 'to be' is in the past.

Teaching. Course books which present the past continuous tend to use disaster situations like earthquakes or hurricanes because they naturally generate statements like 'I was doing the washing up when it struck.' In fact, you can exploit this when practising the form, by getting students to talk about what they were doing when events like the 1981 earthquake happened, or when Italy won the World Cup, or when the last Mafia bombing occurred. It might be interesting to ask students the difference between the following two sentences:

> **When we arrived, Giovanni was making coffee.**
> **When we arrived, Giovanni made coffee.**

Students should see the difference even if they simply translate into Italian.

Problems. There are virtually none, because the structure of a sentence like **I was waiting for the bus when I saw Paolo** is almost identical in Italian. There may be some argument as to whether **I was waiting** is best translated as *aspettavo* or *stavo aspettando* but the concept will be clear. As for the present continuous, there are stative verbs which are never used in this tense.

Present perfect (simple)

Meaning. The present perfect always involves some sort of link with the present even though the action happened or started in the past. It is often divided into three separate usages for ease of teaching, although a particular example may frequently fall into more than one category, or scarcely any at all.

The three 'classic' usages are:

- Experience/indefinite time. In this usage, the action described happened at an unspecified point in the life of the subject. When it happened is not important; the fact that this person has had this experience is what matters. 'Ever' is often included in questions of this type (**Have you ever tried Guinness?**).
- Unfinished past. This is when an action or state began in the past and continues in the present (**I've known Maria for two years**).
- Present result. In this case the action described is completed and in the past (often the recent past), but it has an importance or result in the present (**I've spilt wine on the carpet** – here the present importance is that the wine is still there on the carpet and someone had better clean it up). 'Just' is common in this usage.

Some textbooks talk about a 'news' or 'recent events' usage (**Sabrina's had a baby**) or a 'changes' usage (**Loredana's lost a lot of weight**). In all cases, however, there is a contrast between the past and the present.

Form. The present perfect simple is made up of the auxiliary 'has/have' plus the past participle, which is the third form of the verb on the lists of irregular verbs which are often found in the back of textbooks. Regular verbs form the past participle by adding 'ed' to the verb stem.

The negative and interrogative are made, as in other tenses, by adding 'not' or 'n't' to the auxiliary for the former, and inverting subject and auxiliary for the latter.

Teaching. Because this is quite a complex area, it is advisable to introduce students to the different usages one at a time and to leave the overview until they have got a feel for it.

To teach the first of the usages mentioned above (experience/ indefinite time), a common procedure is to list a series of experiences which students may have had (going to America/ England/France, living abroad, driving a Ferrari) and then to get the class to discuss what they have or have not done.

For the second usage (unfinished past) you can get them to write down someone they know, a possession they have, the place where they live, the job they do, etc, and then have them ask each other questions beginning 'How long . . .' for each of the items on the list. Make sure they do use the present perfect here, because it is not natural for an Italian and it will seem wrong to them.

The third usage (present result) can be practised by showing students pictures of people who have obviously just done something – for example a man taking a cake out of the oven, or a woman coming out of a shop with a big package in her hand. These examples should produce correct sentences in the present perfect (**He's made a cake** and **She's (just) bought something**).

The fact that 'when' is not significant in any of these usages is vitally important, and you will need to underline it again and again.

Problems. There are many. This is because there is no corresponding form in Italian to cover all these situations. It takes practice and a lot of exposure before students start to understand when the present perfect is required.

In Italian the *passato prossimo* looks like the present perfect because it is made up of *avere* (have) and the past participle, but in fact its use is very different. It is worth telling students this from a very early stage.

There are two major conceptual problems. First, English uses the present perfect where Italian uses the present:

> *Lavoro qui da anni.* (Italian present) – **I've worked here for years.**

This is the 'unfinished past' usage already mentioned, and while students may accept it in theory, they will rarely use it spontaneously.

The second problem is the difference between the simple past and the present perfect:

> *Sono stato in Australia.* – **I've been to Australia.**
> *Sono stato in Australia l'anno scorso.* – **I went to Australia last year.**

The crucial point is whether or not we are interested in 'when'. Italians take a long time to accept that you cannot use the present perfect if you mention or even think about 'when'. In Italian the *passato prossimo* can be used indifferently for both.

Another problem is the fact that Italian uses *essere* (to be) as the auxiliary in the past for verbs of movement and change of state. This fact leads students to say things like:

> **I am gone to Pisa.** (*x*)
> **He is become fat.** (*x*)

Present perfect continuous

Meaning. In many instances this is the same as the simple present perfect. For example, in the 'unfinished past' usage (see above) the following are more or less the same:

> **I've lived in Rome for 3 years.**
> **I've been living in Rome for 3 years.**

In the case of 'present result' there is a distinction. Compare these two sentences:

> **I've been writing letters all day (and now I'm sick of it).**
> **I've written 10 letters (and here they are, finished in front of me).**

Both have a present result, but the first is emphasizing the activity itself, not necessarily completed, while the second mentions, and is concerned with the tangible result (10 letters) of a completed action. Also, the continuous implies a continuous or repeated action, while the simple merely states that it has been completed. Thus, unless you were some sort of masochist, it would be impossible to say:

> **I've been cutting my finger. (*x*)**

Form. 'Have/has been' plus present participle. Questions are formed in the same way as in the present perfect simple, while the negative is quite rare.

Teaching. Because the differences between the present perfect simple and continuous are often very subtle, you can limit yourself to straightforward examples with all but the keenest and most advanced students. As a rule of thumb, it is useful to explain that when length of time is mentioned, the continuous is preferred, otherwise the simple is fine.

To practise the 'present result' usage, pictures of people who have obviously just been doing something can serve as good prompts.

Problems. The main problem will be that people have had such a hard time getting to grips with the present perfect simple that they will throw up their hands in dismay when they see that there's a whole new dimension to the business. If the simple is difficult to translate, the continuous is nigh-on impossible. The distinctions do not exist in Italian, or, if they do, they are not expressed by the verb form.

Remember that stative verbs (see above) stay in the simple anyway.

Past perfect

Meaning. To describe an action happening before another action already in the past (**Giorgio had finished his homework when his girlfriend rang**).

Form. The auxiliary 'had' plus the past participle. Negative and interrogative as above.

Teaching. To help students recognize its use, ask them to tell you the chronological order of events in a sequence such as:

> **He ate his dinner and started thinking about the day. He had left home late. That was why he had driven too fast and then been stopped by the police. He looked at the speeding fine on the table and scowled.**

It should become clear that the past perfect verbs all happened before the simple pasts, and yet the order of narration is mixed.

Problems. There are few – the *trapassato* in Italian corresponds very closely. As with the present perfect there may be confusion with verbs like 'go', 'come', etc, which would take 'to be' as the auxiliary in Italian.

Futures

Meaning. There are several ways of referring to the future in English. The three most common are with 'will', 'going to', and the present continuous.

To understand the meaning of each form it will be helpful to create a situation:

A boyfriend and girlfriend are arguing about where to spend their summer holidays. Finally, in exasperation, the girl suggests having separate holidays. 'OK,' says the boy, 'we'll have separate holidays.' Later that day he tells a friend, 'We're going to have separate holidays.' So they each make travel and accommodation arrangements at different places, and when people ask about their plans for the summer they say 'We're having separate holidays.'

We can see that when the boy uses the 'will' future he is making a decision at that moment. When he says 'going to' he is talking about a decision already made, a plan in his head. When he says 'having' (present continuous) everything is fixed up.

Teaching. Take each one separately at lower levels, contrasting them as you introduce another. Talking about future holidays is often a generative subject with which to explore the futures, especially if you can manage to role-play people deciding, then telling each other about what they have decided. The vital point is that students see the importance of *when* the decision is made.

Problems. Despite the fact that Italian does not make the same distinctions about the future as English, students tend to accept the three forms quite readily as long as they are explained clearly enough. Often students have come across the 'will' future before and are convinced that this is *the* future. Naturally, then, this form tends to be overused.

Another problem is that there are many hopelessly out-of-date teach-yourself English books around which say that 'shall' is used in the first person and 'will' in the rest. There are even some that have 'I shalt', 'thou wilt', etc. Explain that now will is used in all persons and 'shall' is used only in a few set situations (such as suggestions – 'Shall we eat?').

Articles (a, an, the)

Teaching the correct use of articles is a tricky affair, because rules are hard to find and if you do find some they are rarely universal. Some teachers prefer to correct mistakes as they come up and leave it at that, because making students think about articles may just lead to more mistakes.

A commonly quoted rule is 'first time "a", second time "the" ' – meaning that the first time you mention a noun it is new and undefined and so you use the indefinite article 'a', and the second time we know what it is you are talking about so you use the definite article, 'the'.

Unfortunately, it is not this aspect that causes problems for Italians; they will naturally get the right article most of the time when it is just a question of new or old nouns. The problems are more specific. The best way to help students is to draw their attention to the individual differences between Italian and English in the usage of articles (see below). This will probably be more useful than a long exposition of the use of articles:

- No article with abstract nouns. When we talk about 'love' and 'hate', for example, there is no article. In Italian, there is one (*l'amore, l'odio*).
- Indefinite article with jobs and professions. Italian prefers *lui è medico* (he is doctor) unlike English, which needs the 'a'.
- No article for countries and football teams. *L'Italia* is simply Italy, not 'the Italy'.

If you can get your students to avoid these three traps, you'll have achieved more than most.

Comparatives (nicer, more beautiful, etc)

Teaching comparatives is not difficult as long as your students know some adjectives. The most important thing is to show how to make ordinary adjectives into comparatives (see box).

SYLLABLES	ADD	ADJECTIVE	COMPARATIVE
One	'er'	**big**	**bigger**
Two, last letter 'y'	'er'	**happy**	**happier**
Two, not ending in 'y'*	more	**modern**	**more modern**
Three or more	more	**beautiful**	**more beautiful**

*Exceptions include 'quiet'; 'narrow'; 'simple'; and 'clever'.

Notice that when 'y' adds 'er' it becomes 'i' (*heavy – heavier*). Point out that comparatives are always followed by 'than'. In the early stages students might try to substitute 'of' instead of 'than' because Italian uses *di* (*più grande di me* – **bigger than I**).

Another common mistake is to use 'more' even with short adjectives – Italian uses *più* (more) with all adjectives, regardless of size.

A good way to practise comparatives is to give out lists of word groups, like **dog–cat–horse–bird**, or **car–bicycle–motorbike–bus**, and ask students to talk about their preferences. This will naturally bring out the use of comparatives.

Superlatives (the nicest, the most beautiful, etc)

These are usually taught soon after, if not together with, comparatives. They are formed using the same scheme as above, but adding 'est' and 'most' instead of 'er' and 'more'.

A common mistake is to say 'the more beautiful', translating directly from Italian (*il più bello*).

A good practice exercise is for students to draw a map of Italy and then label various points on it with superlative sentences like **the longest river in Italy is . . .**, **the biggest football stadium is . . .**, etc. You can put these on the walls afterwards, for others to look at.

Passive (he was sacked, they are used, etc)

Meaning. The passive is used when the 'doer' of the action is unknown or not important. Obviously, passive verbs can be in any tense, just like 'normal' active verbs.

Form. The form is the verb 'to be' plus the past participle. The tense of the verb 'to be' indicates the tense of the whole passive construction. Hence:

> **the song is played** (present simple passive)
> **the song was played** (past simple passive)
> **the song will be played** (future passive)

Negatives and interrogatives are formed as they are in any verb tense, with an auxiliary. In this case it is 'to be'.

Teaching. The most common way to teach passives is to look at manufacturing processes, crop production or resource development in various parts of the world. It is natural to say **oranges are grown in California** or **the trees are cut down and made into paper** because it is the product not the producer which is of interest. By starting off with the present passive in this way, you can then move on to past passives which are natural when talking about famous inventions, discoveries or designs of the past (find something of interest to your students – the origin of football is often a winner).

You can explore future passives later by looking at future space stations or anything which is going to be made or constructed in the future.

Problems. There are not too many, because Italian forms the passive in a similar way. Technical problems of sentence construction may arise when students have to make passives with tenses that use a lot of 'bits' – for example **I was being operated on** is understandably tricky, as is **It is going to be done**. Help students by showing that, even in complicated cases, it is still only a question of putting 'to be' in the relevant tense and adding the past participle.

Questions

Question forms are undoubtedly one of the hardest areas of the language for Italians to master. Questions in Italian are so simple that all the changes in word order and addition of auxiliaries are often seen as much unnecessary fuss.

Apart from the basic question forms which you will teach when you present verb tenses, there are a few other connected grammar items which spread panic and confusion.

Subject/object questions

The difference between the two questions below is that the first has 'who' as its subject, while in the second 'who' ('whom', more correctly) is the object.

Who killed Bambi?
Who did Bambi kill?

A similar effect is possible using 'what', and while the difference is crystal clear to an English-speaker, to an Italian the two forms look like exactly alike. This is because in Italian they are: both of the above questions are translated as *Chi ha ucciso Bambi?*. Whether it was Bambi doing the killing, or being killed, is indicated by sentence stress, or more probably, by the context.

There is no easy way out of this. You just have to explain it and practise it, frequently and patiently.

Indirect questions

Questions which are embedded in a phrase are called 'indirect'.

INDIRECT	DIRECT
I don't know what time it is.	**What time is it?**
Can you tell me where the bank is?	**Where is the bank?**
I wonder if he owns a car.	**Does he own a car?**

The important thing to notice and to make students aware of is that in indirect questions the central, 'question' part does not have the usual interrogative form. In the above examples we have the normal, affirmative form – 'it is', 'the bank is', and 'he owns', instead of the direct question form shown on the right. Notice also that when there is no question-word like 'what' or 'where', we have to supply 'if' to connect the two halves. This last point is not a problem to Italians because they do the same thing in their language (supplying *se* – if). What is a problem is the word order and use of the auxiliary. In Italian, exactly the same form is used in both the direct and the indirect so they tend to use the normal direct question form in both cases in English too.

Tag questions

These are the little questions that you add to the end of sentences in spoken English (**It's hot, isn't it?**).

Their formation is simple: take the auxiliary used in the

sentence and repeat the subject in pronoun form. Make the tag negative if the sentence was positive and *vice versa* (see below). Of course, we do this without thinking. If we had to think about it we would take considerably longer to produce the right form. So be patient with students – they have to perform quite a few mental operations to arrive at a correct tag question.

SENTENCE	TAG
She's French	**isn't she?**
You've got a car	**haven't you?**
They like me	**don't they?**
I don't smell	**do I?**
He left	**didn't he?**
It can wait	**can't it?**
You wouldn't stop	**would you?**

Tag questions are not a difficult concept, but compared to the Italian *vero?* (true?) they are complicated to form, and so Italians rarely use them. This is understandable because they are an aspect of spontaneous, natural speech, and if you have to stop and think you are no longer spontaneous or natural.

Conditionals

'Conditionals' are sentences which posit a condition, and then tell you the result of that condition should it be filled. In other words, they are sentences containing 'if'.

Form. Although there are dozens of possible forms of if-phrases, they tend to fall into a few categories, and it is these which are usually taught. They are:

> *1st conditional* – **If you come, I'll make some tea.**
> **if** (present), (future)

> *2nd conditional* – **If you came, I'd make some tea.**
> **if** (past), ('would' + verb)

> *3rd conditional* – **If you had come, I'd have made some tea.**
> **if** (past perfect), ('would have' + past participle)

Meaning. The first type is used when you are talking about a clear possibility in the present or future. The second type still refers to the present or future, but the likelihood of this happening is far less – it would be a surprise. The third conditional is confined to talking about the past. It refers to a situation which existed in the past but whose outcome has already been decided and is unchangeable.

Sometimes people talk about the 'zero conditional'. This is used too for things which are always true, when 'if' could equally well be 'when'. It uses the present in both sides of the construction:

> **If you boil water, it turns to steam.**
> **That toy makes a sound if you squeeze it.**

Teaching. To teach conditionals well, you should do them one at a time and practise each one a lot before moving on to the next. To practise the first, a useful scenario is one in which students imagine they are about to go on holiday (they decide where) and they talk about possible problems. One student can ask questions like **What will you do if the weather's bad?**, while the other can respond with something like, **(If the weather's bad,) I'll stay in the hotel and eat pizza.**

A good way to practise the second is to get students talking about what they would do in certain unlikely situations. You could make a list including things like:

> **If you became president . . .**
> **If you saw a ghost . . .**
> **If your English teacher attacked you . . .**

To practise the third conditional, ask students to draw a map of their lives, marking points at which they made important decisions or which they see as turning points. It should be clear from the diagram what happened as a result of these decision points. Then ask them to imagine what would have happened if they had acted differently at those points. They should come up with things like: **If I hadn't met Roberto, I wouldn't have moved to Turin** or **If I had asked for a different teacher, I wouldn't be here now**.

Problems. The three conditionals outlined above correspond well enough to conditionals in Italian for their usage not to be much of a problem. Italians often imagine they are more difficult than they actually are. This is perhaps because Italian requires the use of the subjunctive in the second two types, and so students imagine something equally frightening in English. (In fact English too uses the subjunctive, but students do not notice because most of the time it looks the same as the past tenses.) The trap that Italians most commonly fall into is putting the future after 'if' in the first conditional, as is natural in Italian. Thus they say 'If you will come . . .' instead of the correct 'If you come'.

Sometimes students look at the second conditional, see the apparent past tense, and assume it refers to the past. Point out in your presentation that in conditionals the name of the tense you use does not always correspond to the time you are talking about.

Modal auxiliaries

This is an enormous area of language, which you would never consider teaching all in one go. 'Modals' are verbs like 'can' and 'must' which add meaning, modifying the way in which the main verb is viewed. Thus **I must go**, as well as talking about movement ('go'), also tells us that this movement is obligatory in some way ('must'). The modal auxiliaries you will have to teach are probably the following:

> **can/could**
> **must**
> **may/might**
> **will/would**
> **should/ought to**

Meaning. Several of these have more than one possible meaning. For example 'can'; **she can swim** could mean that she knows how to swim (ability), that her mum has said it's OK (permission), or that it is possible because there is a swimming pool nearby (possibility). The generally accepted range of meanings is:

> *Ability* – **can** (**could** in the past)
> *Advisability* – **should, ought to**
> *Conditional* – **would**
> *Future* – **will**
> *Obligation* – **must**
> *Permission* – **can, may, could**
> *Possibility* – **can, could, might, may, must**

Form. Important points to make to students are:

- Modals have no 's' in the third person singular.
- Negatives are formed without the auxiliary.
- Question forms invert subject and verb – no auxiliary.
- Most have only one tense – the present.

This last point is true only up to a point. If you want to talk about the past, you can add 'have' and put the verb in the past participle (**he could have come, they might have smoked**). For the future no real change is necessary because most modals carry a sense of the future in their basic form: **he can stay** might mean now or at some future time.

Teaching. The secret is to take it slowly, doing one meaning at a time. Except at very high levels, looking at all the different meanings will be more confusing than helpful.

'Will' and 'would' arise with the future and the conditional so there is no point in teaching them again. In fact you might not even want your students to think of them as modal auxiliaries to start with, for fear of making something simple seem complicated.

To teach modals of obligation, ask students to make up lists of rules for behaviour in the classroom, or rules for teachers. For modals of possibility, try putting objects in a bag so that they cannot be seen – then, by touching, students guess what they are. In this situation it becomes natural to say things like 'It might be a clock', or 'It must be a book.'

Problems. Italian has equivalents to most English modals, but they do not always correspond exactly, so sometimes there are mistakes due to translating directly (see below, chapter on 'Specific Italian problems'). 'Might' and 'may' have no equivalents in Italian and so they are underused by students. 'Can' is overused, often where 'may' or 'might' would be better:

That can be correct. I don't know.   (*x*)

Reported speech

Meaning. When someone says **I'm an English teacher**, this is direct speech. If you then go and report what this person said to someone else (**He said he was an English teacher**), this is indirect, or reported speech.

Form. The basic rule is quite simple: move the verb one tense into the past (thus, in the example above, 'am' becomes 'was'). You can demonstrate this very clearly to your students with a chart like the one below (see box). The only complications are that 'will' changes to 'would' (future in the past) and that the present perfect and the simple past both change to the past perfect.

DIRECT SPEECH	REPORTED SPEECH
I love you.	He said he loved her.
I'm waiting.	She said she was waiting.
I worked	He said he had worked.
I have finished.	She said she had finished.
I'll come.	He said he would come.

When the direct speech is a question the word order changes too (see 'Indirect questions', p 153).

Teaching. A good way to practise is to have students listen to an interview, or better still conduct interviews in pairs making notes of important information, and then write up or tell someone else what was said in the interview. This technique practises both reported questions and reported statements.

Something else which it is useful to demonstrate is that some words change automatically when they are reported. For example:

'I'm staying here,' he said. / He said he was staying there.

'I' becomes 'he' or 'she' and 'here' becomes 'there'. Other common word changes are:

you – I, he, she
now – then
this – that
yesterday – the day before
tomorrow – the day after/the next day

Problems. The system is more or less the same in Italian, so there are no great difficulties. Students may forget to change pronouns, etc in mechanical practice but as soon as they see what the language means they will put things right without any help. The use of 'say' and 'tell' is a problem, because no matter how many times you tell people they still produce 'he said me' and 'he told to me'. Also, translating 'tell' as *dire* leads people to say 'I told that I was happy'. Put a big notice on the wall saying

TELL + somebody.   SAY + to + somebody.

You will get plenty of mileage out of it.

FUNCTIONS

While grammar deals with the structure of the language and emphasizes concepts like verbs, tenses and the individual parts of speech, functions generally ignore this type of terminology and examine language in terms of what it is used for (its 'function'). The function of the phrase 'could you . . .' is that of asking someone to do something. But you can perform the same function in other ways – for example, 'would you . . .', 'would you mind . . .', 'will you . . .', etc.

Thus individual functions (asking someone to do something, making suggestions, advising) generally have more than one form of expression; in other words they have several 'exponents'. The difference between the exponents is often one of register, or degree of formality. Taking the example above, it is clear that 'would you mind . . .' is used in circumstances different from the simple 'will you . . .'.

In the teaching of functions, students are generally asked to remember certain phrases without going into their grammatical structure. Thus 'would you mind . . .' is not presented as the conditional form of the verb 'mind', but quite simply as a rather formal exponent of a particular function.

The functions covered below are those usually found in course books and they are, by no coincidence, the most useful in everyday life. With each function I list exponents, associated exponents (possible responses), potential problems, and notes on teaching. The lists of exponents are by no means complete – most functions can be expressed in dozens of ways and you should not hesitate to change or substitute any you do not like.

Note that, even though some functions may have six or more possible exponents, this does not mean that you should try to teach all of them to low-level classes. For beginners and elementary students, choose the most common, if possible with neutral register, and just concentrate on those.

Advising

Exponents

> **You should . . .**
> **You ought to . . .**
> **(If I were you,) I'd . . .**
> **Have you thought of . . .**
> **It might be a good idea to . . .**

Associated exponents include:

> **Yes, good idea!**
> **You could be right.**
> **OK. I'll try that.**
> **Yes, but . . . (give reason).**
> **No, that's impossible!**

Problems. 'Should' and 'ought to' are both rather strong if used on their own. In English we tend to soften them by saying 'perhaps' or 'I think' first.

Remember, if you teach 'have you thought of . . .', to point out that it takes the '-ing' form, not the infinitive.

Italians will be tempted to use 'must' in this context, which is possible in Italian but not in English (it sounds far too imperious).

Teaching. Use genuine or invented problem-pages from magazines and ask students to write answers to the letters.

Ask students to think of a problem they have, present it to the class and ask for ideas and advice on how to resolve it.

Get students to prepare an advice sheet for people coming to Italy on holiday.

Apologizing and complaining

Exponents

> **I'm (awfully) sorry but . . .**
> **I'm afraid . . .**
> **I'm sorry I . . .**

Associated exponents include:

> **That's all right.**
> **Don't worry.**
> **Never mind.**
> **Oh no! You idiot!**
> **I'll see to it immediately.**

NB. In English, apologies and complaints often take the same form, and, because they are both quite limited language areas, they can usefully be taught together or in consecutive lessons.

Problems. It is important that students see the difference between apologies for things that are known and for recent mishaps not yet known. For example:

> **I'm sorry I didn't come to the party.**
> **I'm sorry. I've spilt wine on the floor.**

In the first case the simple past is used; in the second, the present perfect. Many teachers just concentrate on the second as the first presents no problems for Italians.

Notice that 'but' is often included after 'I'm sorry' to introduce the unpleasant part, be it an apology or a complaint.

Teaching. Ask students to prepare dialogues between an irate hotel guest and the manager. Invent a list of things to complain about and get them to act it out, with the manager apologizing and trying to put things right.

Other productive situations include: in a disco, someone treads on your toe and spills beer on you; at the travel agent, you have just returned from a terrible holiday; in a restaurant, terrible service, food, etc.

Greetings

Exponents

Hi/Hello
Good morning/afternoon, etc
How do you do?
How are you?
Good bye/bye/see you

Associated exponents: note that the correct response to most of the above is simply to repeat what has been said to you. The only exception is 'How are you?':

Very well thank you.
Fine, thanks.
Not bad.

Problems. There is often confusion between 'How do you do?' and 'How are you?'. Impress on students that the first is simply a formal equivalent of 'Hello', and, despite its form, is not really a question. The second *is* a question and at least ostensibly refers to their state of health.

Greetings above all reflect differences of register, and right from the start students should be aware of which are formal, which neutral and which friendly.

More confusion arises from the differences in greeting people you do not know and those you do know – 'Nice to meet you' becomes 'Nice to see you' and 'How do you do?' is not used at all after the first meeting.

Teaching. The best way to demonstrate all the differences mentioned above is to use prepared dialogues for people in formal and informal situations greeting people they do know and people they do not know. Then get students to tell you the differences.

To practice, set up role-play situations at a party or business meeting.

Make sure students get the hang of basic friendly greetings by asking everyone to say 'hello' to each other at the start of a few lessons. To make it more interesting, tell them to imagine that they are businessmen, royalty, children, Hell's Angels – anything to make them vary the way they say hello.

Introducing people

Exponents

> **(Tommaso) this is Albert.**
> **(Tommaso) I'd like you to meet Albert.**

Associated exponents include:

> **How do you do?**
> **Pleased to meet you.**
> **Hello/Hi!**

Problems. This area is closely connected to that of greetings, and it is likely that both functions would come in the same lesson. As with greetings, it is important to emphasize the register of the three responses (formal, neutral and friendly, in that order).

Obviously there are other ways of presenting somebody, but to avoid confusion it is best to stick to two like those above. Look out for mistakes like 'She is Laura', which reflects Italian usage.

Teaching. As for 'Greetings', above.

Inviting

Exponents

> **Would you like to . . .**
> **Do you want to . . .**
> **(Drink?)**

Associated exponents include:

> **I'd love to.**
> **That'd be great.**
> **Yes, OK.**
> **Sorry, I can't. I'm (doing something or other).**

Problems. A common mistake is to say 'Do you like . . .' instead of 'Would you like . . .'. Point out during presentation that the first is asking whether you like something in general. It is not an invitation like the second.

Also, make sure that students realize that the 'Do you want . . .' form is very informal and should not be used unless you are talking to a friend.

When refusing invitations, some students will just say 'Sorry, I can't' and leave it at that. Indicate that this would be considered rather rude. People generally give reasons when they refuse.

Teaching. Give everyone a diary page for a week and a list of seven things to do (disco, tennis, cinema, etc). Tell students that they have to fix appointments with people to do the things and to fill in the details in their diary. In the resulting activity everyone should have a chance to invite, accept and refuse invitations.

An alternative to the above is to do the same exercise, but with students writing notes to each other, with you acting as postman.

Offering

Exponents

> **Shall I . . . ?**
> **I'll (do it, if you like).**

Associated exponents include:

> **Oh, thank you.**
> **Yes, that would be good.**
> **Well, that's very kind.**
> **No, it's all right (thanks).**

Problems. The word 'shall' may be new to some students, and, as it does not occur very often except in this situation, they are likely to forget it quickly. It also has no equivalent in Italian. The offer **Shall I ring the police?** in Italian is the same as 'Do I ring the police?' (*Chiamo la polizia?*), so look out for mistakes like this, or even 'I ring the police?'

Sometimes students can take some convincing that 'I'll . . .' can be an offer. They simply see it as a future, which is correct grammatically but at times its function is undeniably an offer. A good example is when people are planning something together. In this situation, to offer services, they will say 'I'll make the sandwiches' just as frequently as 'Shall I . . .'.

Note that these exponents are for offering to do something. When you offer *something* to someone it is different. As with invitations, 'Would you like . . .' and 'Do you want . . .' are most common here.

Teaching. Prepare a set of cues with things like 'carry a heavy box', 'look desperately for something' or 'try to start your frozen car' written on them. Give the cues to one half of each pair of students, and get him or her to act out the situation, while the other partner has to offer help, which is either accepted or refused.

Tell students to form groups of four and talk about the organization of an event (a party, a class sports day, a theatre performance, for example). Tell them that everybody is to play a role in the organization and that they have to volunteer to do things. As they are discussing, go round listening and giving points to everyone who uses the correct exponent.

Requesting

Exponents

> **Can you . . . ?**
> **Could you . . . ?**
> **Would you . . . ?**
> **Would you mind . . . ?**
> **Do you think you could . . . ?**

Associated exponents include:

> **Yes, of course.**
> **Certainly.**
> **Sure.**
> **Well, actually . . .**
> **I'm sorry, but . . .**

Problems. The question of register is important here. Point out that the forms become longer and more indirect as they become more formal.

Remember to tell students that all the exponents above take the infinitive, except 'Would you mind . . .'

Notice that all the forms above are for requests in which you ask someone to do something. Sometimes requests involve asking to do something yourself, for example: **Could I open the window?** In this case, the exponents are the same as those for 'permission' (see below). In order not to confuse matters, you might want to ignore these until you look at 'permission'. On the other hand, the chances are that if it comes naturally to a student to use a form with 'I' , they will get it right without thinking. The forms are very similar in Italian.

Teaching. There are many pair activities involving requests. The most simple are along these lines. Everybody has a list of things they are willing to do, and things they are not. Students circulate freely, asking people to do things from the second part of the list. The game continues until students have found people to do at least five things for them.

Another way to practise requests is to set up role-plays in situations such as the morning after a party. The house is a mess, there are hundreds of things to be done; one partner wants to go out while the other tries to get him to help clearing up. Students can write out a dialogue and then perform it for the class, or else (with more advanced students) it can be done *ad lib*.

Suggestions

Exponents

> **Why don't we/you . . .**
> **How about . . .**
> **What about . . .**
> **Let's . . .**

Associated exponents include:

> **That's a good idea.**
> **Yeah, why not.**
> **OK.**
> **Well, actually, I don't like . . . (or whatever the reason is for refusing).**

Problems. Notice the two exponents with 'about' take the gerund, not the normal verb form.

Students may have trouble accepting and using 'What/How about', because in Italian, translated literally, they are meaningless. Emphasize the *function* of the phrase, not its literal meaning. Also be careful that students realize that 'Let's' refers to 'us' (ie the speaker and the person spoken to), so they cannot use it when suggesting that someone do something by themselves.

Teaching. Suggestions can be practised usefully in group discussions. Give each group a list of things to decide – for example: where to go for a group holiday; where to go for a class night out; what food to eat; what film to see. Thanks to the differences in taste which students will inevitably have, there will be a fair amount of suggesting and refusing before a decision satisfactory to all is reached.

Permission

Exponents

> **Can I . . . ?**
> **Could I . . . ?**
> **May I . . . ?**
> **Do you mind if I . . . ?**
> **Would it be all right if I . . . ?**

Associated exponents include:

Of course.
Certainly.
Sure.
Well, actually . . . (reason why not).
No, not at all.

Problems. 'May' is very formal, and it is arguable whether students will ever need to use it. In any case, they will need to know it to understand if not to use. There is no equivalent in Italian, so it will generally be used with reluctance as students feel unsure of what they are saying.

Notice that for the question 'Do you mind . . . ?', 'yes' and 'no' have the opposite value to that which they have with the other exponents.

Students naturally shy away from anything long (like the last two listed above), but they will sound too direct and brusque if they do not use them when asking something difficult or unusual.

Teaching. A good way to practise the different registers when asking permission is to give everyone in the class a new identity. This can be anything from the Queen of England to a 6-year-old schoolboy. Students then ask each other permission to do things in an appropriate form.

12 Specific Italian problems

This chapter is divided into three sections: 'Pronunciation', 'Grammar', and 'Other'. Pronunciation and grammar are two areas where rules and patterns tend to be transferred by the student from his or her own language to the new one, in what is called 'mother tongue interference'. Sometimes English and Italian are similar enough for this not to be a problem, sometimes they are not. The points which follow are largely examples of when this transference is not possible because the two languages are starkly divergent. In the 'Pronunciation' section, two of the problems listed have already been used as examples in the chapter dedicated to teaching pronunciation, and so only a passing reference is made. The grammar section is similarly a corollary to the chapter on 'Teaching grammar and functions' and contains items which are not central to syllabi but consistently cause problems to Italians.

The final section, 'Other', contains every other classic Italian mistake which I can think of. They are mostly examples of literal translation from Italian or words and phrases with shades of meaning which differ from the apparent Italian equivalent. Throughout the chapter, hints on how to deal with the problems are given where possible. Sometimes, however, there is nothing to do but correct the mistake when it happens, and be prepared to spend more time explaining why something is wrong.

PRONUNCIATION

'*Th*.' The fact that this sound does not exist in Italian means that people will often substitute a 't', a 'd', or a 'z' when speaking. Italians find the tongue position, with the tip between the front teeth, strange and uncomfortable. Usually they can produce the sound when asked to, but it is forgotten as soon as they return to spontaneous speech.

The difficulty is further complicated by the fact that there are in fact two variants of the sound: unvoiced, as in 'think' /θ/ and voiced, as in 'those' /ð/.

You might decide that the whole business is not worth the trouble it would cause to teach it. In fact, for communication purposes the correct pronunciation of 'th' is often not important. If you do want to teach it, the first step is to draw attention to the difference. If students have problems producing the different sounds get them to:

(1) Position the tip of the tongue between the front teeth.
(2) Blow air out to produce /θ/.
(3) Continue to blow, but at the same time make a buzzing noise. This should produce /ð/ as in 'that'.

Finally, practise with lists such as the following.

/θ/	/ð/
think	that
three	they
thin	these
through	the

Ghost vowels. The common caricature of Italian speech makes much of this habit of adding vowels, especially at the end of words. For example,

> **I don't-a want-a to drink-a this-a**
> **A big-a, bad-a man-a . . .**

This is because Italians pronounce final consonants more fully than is natural in English, where final sounds are often not 'released'. Try saying 'foreign' and 'foreigner' and you will see that the final 'n' is pronounced fully only in the second case. An Italian, however, when saying the former, may sound almost as if he or she is saying the latter.

To help rectify this habit, take a word ending in 'p','b','t','d','k' or 'g'. Ask students to start saying the final consonant, and then freeze before it is finished. You will probably have to demonstrate before this is clear. If they can do this, they will start to get the feel of how these are pronounced at the end of a word.

Bad/bed. Italian learners tend to pronounce 'bad' as if it were 'bed'; that is, they replace /æ/ with /e/. In fact, the wide-mouthed 'a' does not exist in Italian.

To get them to produce it better, it might be useful to point out that for /æ/ the tongue is at its lowest possible position in the mouth, whereas for /e/ it is a little higher.

'*H*'. The sound itself presents few problems to Italians, new though it is. The problem is that it is frequently dropped when it should be pronounced, and pronounced when it should not be. To get students used to saying aitches, ask them to whisper a series of vowel sounds to you. This should produce the soft effect of a correctly pronounced 'h'. Remember that a piece of tissue held in front of the mouth should not move if the 'h' is correct.

Schwa. This is very rarely used by Italians because it does not exist in their language (see p 132).

Grin/green. In Italian the vowel sound in 'grin' does not exist. All 'i's are pronounced longer, more like the ₋ound in 'green' (see p 131).

GRAMMAR

Subject pronouns. In Italian subject pronouns are frequently missed out; the form of the verb tells you who is doing it, and so a pronoun is unnecessary. As a result, students will often write 'go to Rome' without specifying who. This type of mistake is common with beginners.

'*To*' *for purpose.* Often the Italian word *per* can be translated as 'for' (*Questo è per te* = **This is for you**). So when Italians come to say *Sono venuto per aiutarti* (**I've come to help you**), instead of putting 'to' between the verbs they put 'for'. This is something which must be corrected again and again.

Short answers. English makes frequent use of short answers involving auxiliary verbs:

Do you like it?	**Yes, I do.**
Did he come?	**No, he didn't.**
Will they win?	**Yes, they will.**

Italian says simply 'Yes' or 'No' and either leaves it at that or adds the complete verb again:

Ti piace?	*Sì,(mi piace).*
E venuto?	*No, (non è venuto).*
Vinceranno?	*Sì, (vinceranno).*

The tendency, then, is to do the same in English. Watch out for mistakes like 'Yes, I like'.

To want to. Italians may often say things like **I want that he goes**, because this structure is usual in Italian, whereas 'want' followed by an object and then an infinitive is not.

Also, the fact that English uses 'would like' as a polite form of 'want' causes confusion because the Italian *vorrei* is in fact the conditional form of *volere* (want).

Prepositions. Students make repeated mistakes with prepositions, partly because their logic is very well hidden and also because they are inevitably thinking of what the preposition would be in Italian.

Place and movement. Some of the commonest mistakes are:

I go in England. (*x*)
He comes at home. (*x*)
We live to Rome. (*x*)

To avoid this type of mistake, students must realize that in English prepositions can be of 'place' or of 'movement', and they are two distinct groups. Thus, a verb of movement ('come', 'go', etc) cannot be followed by a preposition of place. Conversely, a non-movement verb cannot be followed by a preposition of 'movement' as in the examples above. This distinction does not exist in Italian.

Some common prepositions of place are: 'in', 'on', 'next to', 'opposite', 'above', 'below', 'in front of', 'behind', 'near', 'at'. And of movement: 'to', 'from', 'into', 'onto', 'under', 'over', 'through', 'across', 'past', 'along', 'out of'.

As part of the verb. Where English uses a few simple verbs and adds prepositions to modify meaning, Italian often has completely different verbs for each shade of meaning. So, when trying to express simple ideas of movement, students often ignore the simple verb and preposition which English prefers. Illustrate this to students, pointing out examples such as the following:

go up	*salire*
go down	*scendere*
go across	*attraversare*
go out	*uscire*
go round	*girare*
go past	*(sor)passare.*

At the end of questions. Questions such as **What are you thinking about?** and **Who is she talking to?** seem strange to Italians because the prepositions are left hanging. Students will be more used to the Latinate structure, which puts prepositions in front of what they refer to (in these cases 'what' and 'who'). The result is some rather stilted sounding questions.

Each other/themselves. In Italian *Si guardano* can mean both **They**

look at each other and **They look at themselves**. When talking about a reciprocal action (the former) students often use the reflexive form (the latter).

Should/shall. Many Italians have been taught that 'shall' and 'should' are used in the first person of the future and conditional verb forms. While strict grammarians might still agree, it is more usual in current English to use 'will' and 'would' in all three persons. Exceptions to this are when making offers and suggestions, when 'shall' is retained – for example:

Shall I open it for you?
Shall we have a party tomorrow?

Should (obligation). In English, to express mild obligation or when giving advice, the form 'should' is often used. In Italian the conditional form of 'must' (*dovere*) is used. This difference, along with the previous problem outlined, creates a good deal of general confusion about what 'should' actually means. As a result, students shy away from using it, and stick to 'must' which they feel safe with, but which is often too strong.

Mustn't/don't have to. In current Italian, both these concepts are expressed in the same way (the negative of *dovere*), and so students may well say **You mustn't pay for the book** when what they mean is that it isn't necessary, or he 'doesn't have to'. The main problem here is that, having one form covering two meanings, Italians do not always realize immediately that there is a real difference. They will probably need to see many examples before this truly sinks in.

Double negatives. Italian students tend to use too many negative words, because in Italian it is acceptable to have more than one in a sentence. *Non è venuto nessuno* literally means **Nobody didn't come**. Explaining the logic will help them accept the rule even if it does not ensure they always remember it.

Word order. Italian word order is more flexible than English where the order 'subject – verb – object' is usual. Mistakes such as '. . . then arrived Giovanni and Paolo' are common, and they reflect the corresponding Italian form (*poi sono arrivati Giovanni e Paolo*).

Uncountables. There are several nouns which in English are uncountable and in Italian are countable. This leads to mistakes where students put an article where it is not required, or pluralize nouns which are always singular – for example, **Can I have an information?** and **Alfredo has black hairs**. See the box below for the most common.

ENGLISH	COMMON MISTAKES
Advice	**an advice, advices** (*x*)
Furniture	**a furniture, furnitures** (*x*)
Hair (on head)	**hairs** (*x*)
Homework	**homeworks** (*x*)
Information	**an information, informations** (*x*)
News	**a news, the news are . . .** (*x*)
Travel	**a travel** (*x*)
Trouble	**a trouble** (*x*)

OTHER

Phrasal verbs. Italians have problems producing phrasal verbs not only because they are numerous and confusing, but also because there often exists a Latinate English word which looks like the Italian word. Students naturally go for what looks and sounds familiar, underusing the 'difficult' phrasal verbs, which are in fact far more common in current English.

There is no easy way around this problem. All you can really do is, over time, try to introduce the most common ones to students in small batches. Although it is tempting just to give out a list and say 'learn 'em', it will probably be counterproductive and you will only succeed in scaring people off altogether.

Following on from this, at least at lower levels, you will be well advised not to refer to 'phrasal verbs' at all. That just gives people something to worry about. Treat each one you come across as a normal vocabulary item, and point out that it is not complete without the preposition. 'Look for', 'look at' and 'look after', for example, should be seen as completely separate items, as they are in Italian: *cercare, guardare* and *curare*. When students have come across two or three with the same base verb, you can draw attention to the different meanings which different prepositions bring to the verb.

Questions which ask for description. The following four questions cause untold confusion for Italians:

What's Massimo like?	*Com'è Massimo?*
What does Massimo like?	*Cosa piace à Massimo?*
What does Massimo look like?	*Com'è Massimo (di aspetto)?*
How's Massimo?	*Come sta Massimo?*

As you can see, the first question (about Massimo's character), when translated literally from Italian, becomes the fourth one (about his health). The second question (about his preferences) is often what is understood when students hear the first. They very rarely produce the first because it is so unlike any Italian question structure, and they forget that 'like' has two meanings (*piace* and *come* in Italian). The third question simply serves to confuse matters all the more.

Be prepared to launch into this explanation whenever it crops up (and it crops up regularly). You will have to go through it at least two or three times before people start to remember.

Bring/take/fetch. All three of these verbs can be expressed by just one in Italian (either *portare* or *prendere*), which simply means to 'transport' or 'carry' something in any direction. The important thing is to show how 'bring' implies movement towards the speaker; 'take' is away, and 'fetch' is away and then back again.

The diagram below may be useful in demonstrating the different meanings.

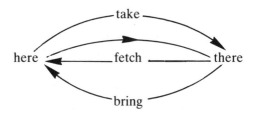

How long. The equivalent in Italian translates literally as 'how much time' (*quanto tempo*) and so students say this, or a mixture – **How long time?** (*x*)

Remind/remember. The same verb is used for both of these in Italian, and so 'remind' is often ignored. Show that with 'remind' two people are involved in the action, whereas with 'remember' there is only the speaker:

Tommaso remembered to phone.
Mari reminded Tommaso to phone.

Make/do. Both of these are covered by the verb *fare* in Italian, and students often use the two English verbs interchangeably. While the difference is in fact vague at times, the general rule is that 'make' involves creating or constructing something, and 'do' refers to the simple completion of an action:

Do the washing.

Do what you want.
Make a table.
Make a mess.

The difference between 'do a puzzle' and 'make a puzzle' should not be too hard to grasp, and it neatly highlights the two meanings. It will not be hard to find exceptions to this rule, or cases where it is meaningless. However, it is a useful starting point, and gives students a guideline.

Having established the rule, expressions like 'do a favour' and 'make love', where the logic is hard to see, will have to be learnt as set phrases.

Make/let. The difference between **They let Manuela come** and **They made Manuela come** is not clear in Italian, in which both are usually translated with *fare*. The crucial difference to get across is that in the first statement Manuela wanted to come, while in the second she did not. You might want to tell students that the implied meaning is one of allowing (*permettere*) and forcing (*constringere*) someone to do something.

Seem/look/look like. The first problem here is one of structure. 'Seem' and 'look' are usually followed by adjectives, while 'look like' takes a noun. In Italian the equivalents (*sembrare*, *parere*) can take both.

The second is one of meaning: 'seem' refers to the general impression given by a person or thing; 'look' and 'look like' refer exclusively to appearance. This distinction is far less marked in Italian and consequently the three possibilities tend to be confused.

Get dressed/dress/wear. The difference between the first two and the last of these verbs is often confused by Italians, as the words are all mentally translated as *indossare*, which can mean both putting clothes on your body and having them already there. Also, the fact that 'dress' is usually reserved for putting clothes on another person is neglected.

If you want to make the differences clear in Italian use the following definitions:

get dressed	*vestirsi*
dress	*vestire*
wear	*avere adosso (indossare)*

Just to complete the picture, you may want to throw in 'put on' as well, as in **He put on his jacket**. This is usually *mettere* in Italian, but gets translated as one of the three above.

So/like this. Students will often say things like **I don't like my hair so** when they mean 'like this'. They are translating *così* in Italian which *is* sometimes 'so' in English but not usually with the sense of 'in this way'.

Hi/Bye. Ciao in Italian can be used at the beginning and at the end of a meeting between friends. It is very common, therefore, to hear students shouting 'Bye' to you as they arrive and 'Hi' as they go. Presumably they fix on one of the two and only hear that, whatever you say.

My tactic is to put a big sign on the inside of the classroom door with 'Bye' on it, and another on the outside saying 'Hi'.

Quite/enough. 'Quite' in the sense of 'fairly, but not excessively' and 'enough' are both *abbastanza* in Italian. It is a simple point, but it needs to be made several times, that 'enough' implies sufficiency while 'quite' is somewhere between 'a bit' and 'very'.

False friends. There are a number of words in Italian which *look* like certain English words, but which in fact have different meanings. They crop up so regularly that within a few months of teaching Italians you will know them by heart. The most common are shown in the box below.

ENGLISH	ASSUMED TRANSLATION	ACTUAL TRANSLATION
actually	*attualmente* ('now', 'currently')	*veramente*
annoyed	*annoiato* ('bored')	*infastidito*
argument	*argomento* ('theme', 'topic')	*lite*
cold	*caldo* ('hot')	*freddo*
confident	*confidente* ('trustful')	*sicuro di se*
expensive	*espansivo* ('open'/'warm')	*costoso*
factory	*fattoria* ('farm')	*fabbrica*
fabric	*fabbrica* ('factory')	*stoffa*
finally	*finalmente* ('at last')	*infine*
inhabited	*inabitato* ('uninhabited')	*abitato*
journey	*giornata* ('day')	*viaggio*
noisy	*noioso* ('boring')	*rumoroso*
parent	*parente* ('relative')	*genitore*
polite	*pulito* ('clean')	*educato*
preservative	*preservativo* ('condom')	*conservante*
rumour	*rumore* ('noise')	*diceria*
sensible	*sensibile* ('sensitive')	*razionale/pratico*
sympathetic	*simpatico* ('nice', 'friendly')	*comprensivo*
terrific	*terrificante* ('terrifying')	*fantastico*

13 Teaching business English

Whatever 'business English' might mean to those who ask for and offer it, in Italy it most often means teaching English to business people. The distinction may appear over-fussy, but the idea that someone with little or no knowledge of English can usefully study the small area of the language concerned with business is strangely common.

The fact of the matter is that to do any ESP (English for Specific Purposes) a basic working knowledge of the language is absolutely essential. For people who need English for their work, the ability to build sentences and understand spoken and written English is more important than knowledge of isolated business terms. In short, you need the framework before you put in the details.

What to teach

With students who are still at an elementary level, then, you need to concentrate on the groundwork. Make sure they know how the tenses work, and can communicate adequately both orally and in writing. Of course you can, and should, if possible, present and practise this basic English in business-type situations. You can present the future tenses, for example, through a dialogue between company directors making plans and predictions for the future. Obviously the dialogue will not be authentic though, and the student will not be learning anything specific about 'business English'.

When students approach the intermediate level, you can start doing what might properly be called business English. You can look at how to write different types of business letter, and start to build up the student's knowledge of specifically business vocabulary. Naturally, at the same time you need to continue working on the same skills which general English students need.

Some useful books for teaching business English are given in Appendix 7.

An individual approach

Most teaching of business people in Italy takes place on a one-to-one basis. This should be exploited to the full, because it means that lessons can be built around the precise needs of the student in question.

It is a good idea to do some sort of 'needs analysis' at the start of the course, to define exactly what the student needs to do with English, and to ensure that time is not wasted on things that will never be useful. You can build this into the lesson, making a questionnaire which pushes the student to be specific about his or her individual needs and to give information about his or her company and job. This latter information can be used as the basis for a presentation in English of the company and the student's responsibilities. This will almost certainly be useful in any English-speaking situation in which students find themselves for reasons of work.

Also, encourage the student to bring into class written material from work. By using it in the lessons, for translation, discussion or whatever, you are sure that what you are doing is relevant.

Problems

In many ways business people are terrible students of English: they have no time for homework; they are often tired and preoccupied in lessons; they frequently arrive late or do not come at all; they want rapid results with minimum effort; they often feel very uncomfortable in the position of learner (especially older men).

Given all these negative factors you will often have to settle for much less than you would with regular students. Progress will be slower, concentration weaker, and output less. Basically, all you can do is accept this and be adaptable.

14 Teaching children

Teaching children is in many ways very different to teaching adults. The fact that in state education teachers very rarely teach both indicates how distinct the two approaches are. Thus you, a non-native teacher, may find yourself in a position unusual even for experienced Italian teachers. This is all the more likely as time goes on, because in many private schools teaching kids is a booming area.

To do it well, you need to do more than just adapt slightly your adult teaching methods. You need an approach which takes into account the characteristics which distinguish kids from adults. These are some of the things you should remember when faced with a class-full of children:

(1) They have a great capacity for mimicking sounds.
(2) They are tactile, attracted by movement and strong visuals.
(3) They can learn very quickly (and forget just as fast).
(4) They have a limited attention span.
(5) They are interested by activities, not by the language needed to complete them.
(6) They have little notion of or interest in grammar as such.
(7) They need to feel they are doing well.

Mimicking sounds. The first of these points, the capacity to reproduce accurately what they hear, is a major help to the teacher of children. It means that drilling and chanting can be extensive, and you need have little fear of the embarrassment and boredom which it often induces in adults. It also means that pronunciation will often be better among your kids than it is among higher-level adults.

Movement and visuals. If you remember that far back, you will probably recall that sitting still for any length of time is quite an ordeal for a child. Indeed, children across the board tend to be constantly bursting with energy. For this reason it is important to work into your lessons a number of activities (games) which involve movement, and the chance to let off some steam. What is more, children are stimulated by touching and seeing real solid objects. Exploit this, use real things in your lessons so that students can handle them and associate their feel to the language your are trying to teach. Similarly, use their attraction for bright colours and pictures by using lots of visual aids. And try to make everything you use look attractive visually; children get very turned off by bad photocopies and plain looking worksheets.

Quick learners. Children have the ability to learn large chunks of information very quickly and this is an obvious bonus in language learning. By using a lot of songs you can exploit this fact, while linking it to the natural pleasure which people get from rhythm and melody. Another reason songs tend to work well with children is that they sometimes feel less self-conscious than adults about singing, and consequently they get much more from the experience. The flip-side of this skill at rapidly picking up language is that it can go again with equal rapidity. Don't be too upset if you find that something you thought you had taught them seems to have disappeared without trace. The fact that it went in once is something in itself. Also, be prepared for very irregular progress – kids learn in fits and starts, and stubborn pushing by the teacher will do little to alter this. They learn when they are ready and all you can do is make sure there is something there for them to learn when they are ready.

Limited attention span. One thing you cannot count on with kids is motivation. Adults generally choose to learn English and so will usually do what you ask on the understanding that it will help them with the language. Kids, on the other hand, are usually sent to learn by their parents. Consequently you have to stimulate them constantly if you want to get anything done.

The word 'constantly' in the last sentence is important because children lose interest in most activities (no matter how hard you have worked to prepare them) after 10 or 15 minutes. This means that you have to change activity at least 4 or 5 times in an hour, and, as well as this, you should think hard about 'pace' and 'focus'. Move their attention from you, to themselves, to objects, to books, to tapes and so forth, and intersperse fast-moving games with slower, more thoughtful exercises.

Activities. Short-lived as your students' attention may be, it is intense while it lasts. If they are involved in an activity, all other considerations fall by the wayside, and this often includes speaking in English. Be prepared to be rather more lenient about this than you would with adults. If you speak any Italian, you may also want to use it (especially with real beginners) for giving instructions and checking understanding.

Grammar. Teaching grammar is not something you can do very much of with young children – at least not ostensibly. If they are unaware of the structures of their own language, it is too much to expect them to grasp those of another. As a teacher you should know what aspects of grammar you want the children to become familiar with, but present it in a functional aspect. Through activities like games and role-plays they can absorb what we would call 'grammatical knowledge' without being aware of it. If at some point students ask why we use one form here and another there, you can give them an explanation, but in the simplest of terms. Students who have asked for information are more likely to retain it than those who have it presented to them as a slice of 'grammar'. Obviously you should avoid grammatical terminology and make the concept as accessible as possible.

Encouragement. Nothing makes students do badly like the feeling that they are doing badly. The answer to this is lots of encouragement and praise. Always give credit to any student who is trying to use English, in whatever form and however badly. An extension of this is not to neglect giving praise to weaker students – teacher approval is a very strong carrot for most kids, and most of all for those who feel a little inadequate. Be careful too about the difficulty of what you ask students to do. Children quickly give up if they perceive something as too difficult. The same is true if it is too easy. It is human nature to want to do more of what you can do well.

Classroom management

Discipline is probably the thing which most worries new teachers of children. Keeping students interested is undoubtedly a very important factor in keeping control, but there are some other things which you can do to minimize the danger of misbehaviour. Here are ten pointers:

- Be strict to start with and *then* ease off if you want. Doing the reverse is practically impossible.
- Decide seating arrangements yourself. This avoids chaos at the start of the lesson and the formation of cliques.
- Use eye-contact to show you are in control. Use body-language too to communicate approval/disapproval.
- Make sure you have everybody's attention before you start any exercise or presentation.

- Make sure students understand what they have to do. Make instructions simple and clear.
- Establish a routine for the start and the end of lessons (eg coats off, sit down, books out, face front, homework ready).
- Don't fuss and give off nervous energy. Look calm and in control.
- Make shouting and displays of anger as rare as possible. The rarer they are, the more effective they will be.
- Find out what disciplinary measures are available to you, and never make a threat you are not prepared to carry out.
- Show no favouritism, and don't let individual students think they are being picked on.

Appendices

Appendices

Appendix 1 | Case studies – using your experience

Lucy Jones grew up in the English Midlands and went to the University of Exeter where she studied French and German. On graduating, she 'messed around' for a time, then did a TEFL course in London and immediately afterwards found a summer job in the north of Italy. The summer job became a full-time one and Lucy ended up staying for four years, moving to Rome for the last two.

Returning to England in 1992, she found a job editing English-language course books with Oxford University Press. She says they gave her the job because of her knowledge of Italian and also French, which she had studied at university. She now works on books destined for the Italian/French state school market. The job involves frequent travel to Italy to talk to teachers, liaising with authors, and coordinating the production of books.

Peter Greenwood studied History at Cambridge Polytechnic and then came to Italy where he worked for a series of private schools in the South before finally starting his own school with two friends. The school did some work for the European Community (now the European Union), organizing language courses for the unem-ployed and through this Peter came into contact with EC training projects in the area. Having decided to move away from straight-forward teaching towards more managerial work, Peter got a job as a local superviser of EC training programmes in southern Italy. After two years here, coordinating language and computer courses, he was invited to Brussels to work as a consultant on the COMETT programme (EU-funded initiatives in education and training in technology).

Martin Cross was born in Ottowa, Canada, and taught English in Japan before coming to Italy. He taught for two years in Rome and then decided to get into translation work.

With a fax, a computer and telephone in his apartment, he can do all his work without moving an inch. He has succeeded in getting a series of regular clients in Japanese and Italian companies, so that he uses both the languages he has learnt. Although the work is insecure, he likes the freedom it gives him, and the fact that there's no middle-man taking most of the money.

For Martin, teaching was a way into Italy. It supported him while he learnt the language, found an apartment, acquired all his documents and explored the possibility of becoming a professional translator. He is currently considering moving to Paris, where he would like to carry on translating and set about learning French.

Pete McMillan was born and bred in a village near Edinburgh, where he also went to university. There he studied French and Italian and spent a year as an English assistant in Verona. After graduating, he decided he wanted to teach Italian, so he did a PGCE (one-year teaching course) and then got a job teaching English in Bologna. He stayed there for two and a half years, using the time to perfect every aspect of his Italian.

In 1990 he went back to the UK and after a little time found a job teaching Italian in a London secondary school. He says the time he spent teaching in Italy not only gave him a real grasp of the language he wanted to teach, but also helped him develop as a teacher. He finds teaching young teenagers in London harder than the adult classes in Italy, but also more rewarding because the kids are more flexible and, when motivated, respond very well to 'communicative' teaching methods.

Annette Benning came to Italy from Sydney, Australia, in 1990. She did a grand tour of Europe, finishing up in Rome where she had already arranged to do the RSA TEFL Certificate course. She passed and immediately found work teaching in a company.

Annette enjoyed her two years teaching immensely, but admits that she never saw herself as a long-term teacher. In 1992 she returned to Australia and started looking for a job in which she could start thinking about a career. She thinks she was wise to leave when she did because otherwise she would have found herself trapped in a job and a country which were not ultimately for her. Arriving back in Australia she found that her two years in Italy were not seen at all negatively by prospective employers. On the contrary, it was perceived as an interesting point in her CV.

Eventually Annette found work with the Australian Film Commission. Italian is not at all important for her work, and while her experience in Italy did not open any doors for her professionally, she does not regret it at all. Her advice to teachers who do not want a career in TEFL is to come, have fun and go home. Don't leave it too late and find you have let other doors close on you.

Appendix 2 | Interviews with two English teachers

Anne-Marie is 27, from Honolulu, and has been teaching English in Italy for four years. At the moment she is living in Rome and working freelance for a school specializing in company courses.

When did you come to Italy, and why?
Well, I first came in 1987 to study at the American University in Rome. That was part of the degree I was doing in Political Science in California. Then I went back, finished my degree and decided I wanted to come back to Italy. I didn't know what I wanted to do – I hadn't really thought about teaching as an option. Anyway, by 1989 I was in Rome again, looking for something to do.

Did you have any teaching qualifications?
No, none at all. In fact I still haven't. Everything I know about teaching I've learnt on the job. I could have done the RSA certificate, but somehow I never got round to it. As long as I stay here it doesn't matter too much, because I've got the contacts to be able to find work. But I think it would be hard if I went anywhere else. I probably wouldn't get into the really good schools without it.

How did you get your first job?
I saw an ad in *Porta Portese* [the Roman classified ads paper] for a bilingual secretary in a language school. When I applied the woman said that that job was taken, but she needed English teachers, so why didn't I do that? I said OK, and started teaching a week later. I had never taught English before and didn't really know what I was doing but I really liked it. So I carried on.

What advice would you give to someone looking for teaching work?
For private lessons, put ads in the papers and at the bookshop too. But if you're a woman don't put your name, or anything that shows you're female. And the first time you meet clients, make sure it's a public place, *not* at your home.

As far as school work is concerned I think that contacts and the teacher grapevine are the best bet. Then there are the English-language newspapers, here in Rome both *Metropolitan* and *Wanted in Rome* are good sources. But still the grapevine is better. If you see other teachers' ads, ring them up and ask for advice.

I've found that, when dealing with schools and directors, persistence pays off. I got my present job (so my boss told me) because I kept ringing up. He was impressed by that, and remembered me when a job came up.

What was your first job like?
It was a small school, but a fairly serious outfit. The work was in the school, with small groups (about 5 or 6) and I suppose it was good really for a first job. Most of the work was in the evening, but that's fairly normal, and the pay was about average as I remember.

What struck me in my first few months' teaching was how it really wasn't that hard. In fact it could even be fun, which I hadn't really expected.

And what about your present job?
It's a pretty good deal, I think. I teach in a large computer company (this is through my school obviously) and I finish at four o'clock, which is great because a lot of people are only starting at that time. My boss is an American and we get on pretty well. The pay is about 27 000 lire an hour, but 20% of that gets taken off for tax [*Ritenuta d'Acconto*].

The negative things are that I'm not on contract, so I haven't got much security. Obviously, holidays aren't paid – that's about two and a half months a year. Also my boss expects a lot from us. He's very professional which is good I suppose, but we have to spend hours filling in reports on lessons, on homework and he wants to know exactly what each student is up to. That's a bit of a drag, but generally he's OK.

What do you think of Italians as students?
Well, I haven't got much to compare them with, but I'd say they're fairly good. They're fun, talkative and not *too* serious, which is good. Businessmen can be a pain. They are often arrogant, it's difficult to tell them they've made a mistake. And they expect you to be at their beck and call. No, but in general they're good, definitely.

Where do you see yourself two years from now?
What a horrible question! Not teaching, quite possibly still in Italy though. For me there's not enough security in teaching English. It's good because you meet so many people, but after four years

I'm a bit tired of having to be 'switched on' all the time when I work. Sometimes I would love to just sit at a desk and be *incognito* for a while. Teaching can be very intimate.

Chris is 26 and has worked for International House since he came to Italy two years ago. He is a New Zealander and has a degree in History from Auckland University.

Why did you come to Italy?
I don't know really. I guess I was kind of fascinated by the place when I came here on holiday and so afterwards I thought I'd try to come back here to live. I looked at how it could be done, and it seemed that teaching was a good way in. It seemed the obvious thing to get a job.

Did you have any teaching qualifications or training?
Yes, well I came to Rome specifically to do the RSA TEFL certificate. I could have done it in New Zealand, but I thought it would be more useful to get a job if I did it here. Since then I've also done a course on teaching children, which was organized through this school.

How did you get your first job?
They offered it to me. I finished the certificate course, and, I don't know, but my name must have been passed down some grapevine and almost immediately the Director of Studies of this school contacted me and offered me the job. Which I accepted – gratefully.

What advice would you give to someone looking for work?
Well, with the certificate I don't think it's that hard. Without, it might be tougher, especially if you haven't got any experience. A friend of mine, an Australian, did the course at the same time as me, and she got a job straight away, no problem. There are plenty of schools that will give you a job, even if you're from outside the EU – as long as you've got the certificate that is.
  If it were me, I'd go through the yellow pages, ring up all the schools and go round there with my CV and qualifications. There's always someone who needs teachers. I suppose if I wanted to go somewhere else in Italy I'd probably go through the IH recruitment agency. Now I can get a reference from an IH school, I think I'd be a more attractive prospect to other IH schools.

What's your present job like?
I work 20 hours a week here. It's teaching adults mostly, in the

school, not in companies. We have group courses at different levels going on nearly all the time, and this makes up the bulk of what I do. Most of the work is in the evening, which is probably the major drawback. Working till ten o'clock ruins your social life.

On the positive side, it's a good school, with a reputation, and everything's pretty well organized. We have plenty of materials and teacher back-up, and the students are usually pretty good. We've got contracts, so we get a fixed salary every month, even in summer and at Christmas when we're not working. I think that's quite unusual.

What were the first few months of teaching English like for you?
I found them really hard. I was really stressed a lot of the time and I found it all a bit overwhelming. I used to spend hours planning lessons and the idea of having more than two a day seemed outrageous. I didn't feel safe in a classroom unless I was armed with piles of photocopies. I think the mistake you make at the beginning is to think too much about you, the teacher, and not enough about them, the students.

My first-ever course was a group of level-one beginners and, despite everything, I thought it was really good. I didn't speak any Italian at that point, and they knew that, so all communication was in English. Since I've learnt Italian I find it very hard to get the amount of Italian used in class down to the level of those first few months.

What do you think of Italians as students?
Pretty good. They can ask some quite personal questions though. And at completely the wrong moments, like in the middle of a listening exercise. I suppose the best thing, which is the same thing I suppose, is that they're always ready to talk, they've always got something to say.

Where do you see yourself two years from now?
I see myself in Italy but not teaching English. Maybe with a shop selling artefacts from the South Pacific.

Appendix 3 Some English schools

Rome

Accademia Americana, Via del Corso 514 (Tel: 06 3201823)
Berlitz, Via di Torre Argentina 21 (Tel: 06 68806951); Viale Giulio
 Cesare 207 (Tel: 06 39726139); Via PL da Palestrina 19 (Tel:
 06 3204624); Via Pasteur 77 (Tel: 06 5920900)
British Council, Via 4 Fontane 20 (Tel: 06 4871060)
British Institute of Rome, Via 4 Fontane 109 (Tel: 06 4881979)
British School, Via Lucullo 14 (Tel: 06 4880333); Viale Europa 55
 (Tel: 06 5921273); Lungotevere Ripa 6 (Tel: 06 5806310);
 Via Cassia 536 (Tel: 06 3350018)
Buckingham School, Via Giovanni Caselli 34 (Tel: 06 5580218)
Inlingua, Via A Salandra 6 (Tel: 06 4742814)
Interco-op, Via IV Novembre 114 (Tel: 06 6785427)
Interlingue, Via Federico Cesi 62 (Tel: 06 3215740)
International House, Dilit, Via Marghera 22 (Tel: 06 4462602); Via
 San Godenzo 100 (Tel: 06 3351140); Viale Manzoni 57 (Tel:
 06 77208218); Viale Etiopia 8 (Tel: 06 86207801); Piazza di
 Villa Carpegna 45 (Tel: 06 6635987)
International Language School, Via Tibullo 10 (Tel: 06 6876801)
King's English, Via Valle Corteno 75 (Tel: 06 896620)
Lead On, Via Montagne Rocciose 62 (Tel: 06 5915521)
New English American Centre, Viale Trastevere 259 (Tel: 06
 5883214)
Oxford Institute, Via Piemonte 127A (Tel: 06 486785); Via degli
 Scolopi 31 (Tel: 06 3057985); Via Morgagni 25 (Tel: 06
 8416994)
PETS (Professional English Teaching Service), Via N Zabaglia 3
 (Tel: 06 5741242)
Teach-In, Piazza S Giovanni in Laterano 18/b (Tel: 06 70497526)
Team Teaching, Via Baldassarre Peruzzi 14 (Tel: 06 5746183)
Training, Via Marocco 3 (EUR) (Tel: 06 5916684)
Wall Street Institute, Piazza S Silvestro 8 (Tel: 06 6793785)

Milan

American & British Institute, Via Gran S Bernardo 18 (Tel: 02 33611570)
American Language Institute, Via G Carducci 12 (Tel: 02 8900011)
Berlitz, Via delle Asole 2 (Tel: 02 86450974)
British Council, Via Manzoni 38 (Tel: 02 782016)
British School, Via Montenapoleone 5 (Tel: 02 780741)
British Institute, Piazzale Cadorna 9 (Tel: 02 72000974); Via Marghera 45 (Tel: 02 48011149)
Canning School, Via Sanremo 9 (Tel: 02 7386404)
HM, Corso Vercelli 35 (Tel: 02 436755)
Inlingua, Via GB Morgagni 5 (Tel: 02 29523524); Via Fabio Filzi 27 (Tel: 02 66985320); Via G Leopardo 21 (Tel: 02 48013374)
International Language School, Corso di Porta Romana 2 (Tel: 02 72002665)
Linguarama Italia, Corso di Porta Vittorio 10 (Tel: 02 5512818)
Linguaviva, Via C di Cristoforis 15 (Tel: 02 6596401)
Multi-Method, Largo Richini 8 (Tel: 02 58304544)
Oxford Institute, Piazzetta Pattari 2 (Tel: 02 72003551); Via Caccialepori 22 (Tel: 02 48706030); Via Campanini 7 (Tel: 02 68986830); Via G Bellini 1 (Tel: 02 48954580)
Person to Person, Via Larga 26 (Tel: 02 8053336)
Wall Street Institute, Corso Vittorio Emmanuele 30 (Tel: 02 76001435); Piazzale Cadorna 15 (Tel: 02 804626); Corso Buenos Aires 77 (Tel: 02 6703108)
Westminster Institute, Via Boccaccio 21 (Tel: 02 48002305)

Naples

British Council, Via dei Mille 48 (Tel: 081 421381)
British School, Via Roma 148 (Tel: 081 5523869)
Cambridge School, Piazza Leonardo 77 (Tel: 081 5560056)
Inlingua, Via Cimarosa 76 (Tel: 081 5782020)
Interco-op, Via Nazionale 75 (Tel: 081 206205)
International House, Piazza Degli Artisti 38 (Tel: 081 5781261)
Oxford Institute, Via Chiaia 149 (Tel: 081 418089)
Wall Street Institute, Via Morelli 2 (Tel: 081 7646642); Piazza Vanvitelli (Tel: 081 5780408)

Appendix 4 | Classroom Italian

Most grammatical terms are very similar in Italian, so it is usually not necessary to translate, except for absolute beginners. However, just for the record, here are the words and phrases which crop up most frequently.

Parts of speech

noun *nome/sostantivo*
pronoun *pronome*
verb *verbo*
adjective *aggettivo*
adverb *avverbio*
article *articolo*
preposition *preposizione*

Tenses

present *presente*
(continuous) (*progressivo*)
present perfect (*no translation; does not exist)*
past *passato*
past perfect *trapassato*
future *futuro*

Other useful words

question *domanda*
answer *risposta*
sentence *frase*
subject *soggetto*

singular *singolare*
plural *plurale*

stress *accento*
syllable *sillaba*
consonant *consonante*
vowel *vocale*

polite *formale*
informal *informale*

opposite *contrario*
like *simile*

Useful phrases

You don't need 'x'   *Non ci vuole 'x'*
'x' is missing   *Manca 'x'*
In pairs   *In coppie*
Put in the right order   *Mettere nell'ordine giusto*
What does that mean?   *Che vuol' dire?*
How do you say 'x'?   *Come si dice 'x'?*
How do you spell 'x'?   *Come si scrive 'x'?*
For example   *Per esempio*
Ready?   *Pronti?*

Appendix 5 Food and drink glossary

Types of pizza

Calzone a normal pizza folded over with ham, tomato and mozzarella inside

Capricciosa with everthing (ie ham, tomato, mozzarella, olives, egg, artichokes, mushrooms)

Funghi tomato, mozzarella and mushrooms

Frutti di mare seafood, such as mussels, prawns and squid

Margherita tomato and mozzarella

Marinara tomato, garlic and oregano

Napoletana tomato, mozzarella and anchovies

4 Formaggi 4 cheeses (mozzarella, gorgonzola, gruyère and fontina)

4 Stagioni '4 seasons', more or less the same as *Capricciosa*, but divided into 4 segments

Pasta sauces

Amatriciana spicy tomato sauce with bits of pork

Arrabbiato straightforward but (very) spicy tomato sauce

Bolognese classic minced beef and tomato sauce

Carbonara with ham and egg

Funghi mushrooms

Panna cream (often together with mushrooms)

Pesto Genovese sauce containing basil, garlic and pine nuts

Pomodoro simple tomato sauce

Ragù larger pieces of meat in a tomato sauce

Vongole hardly a sauce, just a lot of clams in butter on your pasta

Meat and fish (*carne e pesce*)

acciughe anchovies
agnello lamb
anguilla eel
aragosta lobster
baccalà cod
bistecca steak
calamari squid
carpaccio raw beef cut very thin
cervella brain
coniglio rabbit
cozze mussels
fegato liver
gamberetti shrimps
gamberi prawns
granchio crab
lingua tongue
maiale pork
manzo beef
merluzzo cod
ostriche oysters
pancetta bacon
polipo octopus

pollo chicken
polpette meatballs
prosciutto ham
rognoni kidneys
salsiccia sausage (spicy)
sgombro mackerel
sogliola sole
tonno tuna
tacchino turkey
vitello veal
vongole clams

Vegetables (*contorni*)

asparagi asparagus
broccoli broccoli
carciofi artichokes
carotte carrots
cavolfiore cauliflower
cavolo cabbage
cetriolo cucumber
cipolla onion
fagioli beans
fagiolini green beans
funghi mushrooms
insalata salad
lattuga lettuce
melanzane aubergine
patate potatoes
peperoni peppers
piselli peas
pomodoro tomato
spinaci spinach
zucca marrow
zucchini courgettes

Sweets and fruit (*dolci e frutta*)

ananas pineapple
arancia orange
banana banana
ciliege cherries
coccomero water-melon
fichi figs
fichi d'India prickly pears
fragole strawberries

gelato ice-cream
limone lemon
macedonia fruit salad
mela apple
pera pear
pesca peach
tartufo a very superior chocolate ice-cream
tiramisù a sweet coffee-flavoured dessert
torta cake, tart
uva grapes
zabaglione a dessert made from eggs, sugar and Marsala
zuppa Inglese trifle

Drinks (*bevande*)

acqua minerale mineral water (*gasata/non-gasata*) (fizzy/ still)
aranciata orangeade
birra beer
caffè coffee
cioccolata (calda) (hot) chocolate
granita crushed-ice fruit drink
latte milk
limonata lemonade
spremuta freshly squeezed fruit juice
spumante sparkling wine
succo di frutta fruit juice (not fresh)
tè tea
(acqua) tonica tonic water
vino wine
  bianco white
  rosato rosé
  rosso red
  secco dry
  dolce sweet

Other useful words

aceto vinegar
aglio garlic

arrosto roast
ben cotto well-done
bicchiere glass
bollito boiled
bottiglia bottle
brodo soup
burro butter
crudo raw
formaggio cheese
al forno baked
fritto fried
ghiaccio ice
grissini bread sticks

(*alla*) *Milanese* fried in egg and
    breadcrumbs
olio oil
pane bread
panino bread roll/sandwich
patatine fritte French fries
pepe pepper
ripieno stuffed
sale salt
al sangue rare
salute! cheers!
surgelato frozen
zuppa soup

Appendix 6 — Festivals and holidays

National holidays

1 January	New Year
6 January	Epiphany
(varies)	Easter Monday
25 April	Liberation Day
1 May	Labour Day
15 August	*Ferragosto* (Assumption of Virgin Mary)
1 November	*Tutti i Santi* (All Saints)
8 December	Immaculate Conception of Virgin Mary
25 December	Christmas
26 December	Santo Stefano

Other festivals

Most of Italy's religious and traditional festivals are local affairs. Every town and city has a patron saint, and every year when his/her day comes round, the local population turns out to form processions and celebrate with fairs and fireworks.

There are also the *sagre* – seasonal feasts celebrating the harvest or the reaping of a particular local crop or food. They usually occur in towns and villages with a specialist agricultural tradition.

There are two important dates which are celebrated all over Italy. **Carnevale** (date varies between end of February and end of March) usually involves parades and lots of dressing up in costumes and masks. The carnival in Venice is the biggest and most hyped, but there are also big events in Viareggio (Tuscany) and Acireale (Sicily). The **Festa della Donna** (8 March) is a day dedicated to women, which seems to consist mainly of men buying and giving out sprigs of the yellow mimosa to all the women in their lives. Women often go out in groups on a sort of annual 'hen night'.

A Christmas tradition prevalent in many towns (especially in Naples and Verona) is the construction and exhibition of *Presepi* (nativity scenes). These are often highly elaborate affairs, which are worked on for months by craftsmen, specialized in the art.

Some big local festivals

Agrigento	Almond Blossom Festival (February).
Alba	*Giostra delle Centro Torri* – *palio* (horse-race), costume parade and truffle fair (first Sunday in October).
Arezzo	*Giostra del Saracino* – knights jousting (first Sunday in September).
Ascoli Piceno	*Torneo della Quintana* – jousting (first weekend in August).
Asti	Bareback riders in horse-race (third Sunday in September).
Bolzano	Wine festival (second half of March).
Cocullo	Saint Dominic Abate's day. A statue of the snake-covered saint leads procession (6 May).
Florence	Saint John's day. Fireworks and the historic game of football between teams in medieval costume from each quarter of the city (24, 28 June).
Foligno	Knights' jousting competition (second weekend in September).
Gubbio	*Festa dei Ceri*, a race with huge wooden poles to the ancient church (5 May).
Marostica	Chess game with people as pieces in castle yard (second weekend in September).
Milan	Procession of three Wise Men through the city centre (6 January); and *Mercato di Sant'Ambrogio*, a display of locally produced *Presepi* (nativity scenes) throughout December.
Naples	*Festa di San Gennaro*, three times a year a ceremony in the cathedral witnesses the Saint's dry blood turn liquid (first Saturday in May, 16 September, 19 December).
Nocera Tirinese	Procession of self-flagellation (Easter Saturday).
Orvieto	Wine festival (June).
Pisa	*Luminaria*, festival of lights (16–17 June).
Rome	*La Befana*, the good witch of Epiphany has a toy and sweet fair in her honour in Piazza Navona (6 January); also *Festa de' Noantri*, a party/fair in the streets of Trastevere (16–24 July).
Siena	The famous medieval *Palio* horse-race (2 July, 16 August).
Tivoli	Wine festival, when the town's fountains run with wine (second Sunday October).
Venice	*Il Redentore*, a celebration of the end of the Plague in the 16th century – procession of gondo-

las, fireworks, etc (third week in July); also the famous *Regatta* (first Sunday in September).

Ventimiglia   *Regatta* and celebrations (9–10 August).

Appendix 7 Selective bibliography

Italy

Luigi Barzini, *The Italians* (Penguin/Macmillan)
Edward Gibbon, *History of the Decline and Fall of the Roman Empire* (Penguin)
Christopher Hibbert, *Rome: The Biography of a City* (Penguin); *Venice: The Biography of a City* (Grafton); and *Garibaldi and his Enemies* (Penguin)
Valerio Lintner, *A Traveller's History of Italy* (Windrush Press)
William Ward, *Getting It Right in Italy* (Bloomsbury)
The Rough Guide to Italy (Rough Guides)
Let's Go: Italy (Pan/Harvard Students Agencies)

Learning Italian

Teach Yourself Italian (NTC Publishing)
Italian in 3 months (Hugo)
Buongiorno Italia! (BBC Video)

For teaching

Course books – adults

Sue Mohammed and Richard Acklam, *Choice* (Longman) – three-book series from beginner to intermediate level
John and Liz Soars, *Headway* (Oxford University Press) – books from beginner to advanced levels
Michael Swan, *New Cambridge English Course* (Cambridge University Press) – four books starting at beginner and going up to First Certificate
Brian Abbs and Ingrid Freebairn, *Blueprint* (Longman) – three books at beginner, elementary and intermediate levels respectively
Adrian Doff and Chris Jones, *Language in Use* (Cambridge University Press) – two books at pre-intermediate and intermediate levels respectively

Jan Bell and Roger Gower, *Matters* (Longman) – two books at intermediate and upper-intermediate levels respectively

Course books – children

Rob Nolasco, *Window on the World* (Oxford University Press) – three books for young teenagers (beginner, elementary and intermediate)
Colin Granger and Digby Beaumont, *New Generation* (Heinemann) – three books for late teens (beginner, elementary and intermediate)
Julie Ashworth and John Clark, *Stepping Stones* (Collins ELT) – three books (levels for young children)
Snap (Heinemann) – three books (levels for 7–9 year-olds)

Supplementary material

Richard Acklam, *Help with Phrasal Verbs* (Heinemann)
Jill Hadfield, *Communication Games* (Nelson)
Diane Hall and Mark Foley, *Survival Lessons* (Nelson)
Friederike Klippel, *Keep Talking* (Cambridge University Press)
Raymond Murphy, *English Grammar in Use* (Cambridge University Press); *Essential Grammar in Use* (Cambridge University Press)
Mario Rinvolucri, *Grammar Games* (Cambridge University Press)
Wendy Scott, *Are You Listening?* (Oxford University Press) – listening for elementary-level children
Penny Ur, *Grammar Practice Activities* (Cambridge University Press)
Penny Ur, *Discussions that Work* (Cambridge University Press)
Peter Watcyn-Jones, *Pairwork One* (Penguin English) – aimed at pre-intermediate students
Peter Watcyn-Jones, *Pairwork* (Penguin English) – intermediate and above

See also the two very useful series:

Cambridge Handbooks for Language Teachers (Cambridge University Press), General Editor – Michael Swan
Resource Books for Teachers (Oxford University Press), Series Editor – Alan Maley

Business

Brieger, Comfort, Hughes and West, *Business Contacts* (Prentice-Hall) – pre-intermediate
Ken Caster and David Palmer, *Business Assignments* (Oxford University Press)
Vicki Hollet, *Business Objectives* (Oxford University Press)
Leo Jones and Richard Alexander, *International Business English* (Cambridge University Press)

Howard, Williams and Herd, *Business Words* (Heinemann) – intermediate and above
Robert O'Neill, *English Works* (Longman) – elementary level

Videos

Mystery Tour (Oxford University Press) – intermediate
Grapevine (Oxford University Press) – beginner/elementary
Two Days in Summer (Longman) – elementary

Teacher reference

Collins Cobuild English Grammar (Collins)
Jeremy Harmer, *The Practice of English Language Teaching* (Longman)
Geoffrey Leech, *A–Z of English Grammar and Usage* (Edward Arnold)
A. Matthews, *At the Chalkface* (Nelson)
W. Rivers, *A Practical Guide to TESL and TEFL* (Oxford University Press)
Michael Swan, *Practical English Usage* (Oxford University Press)
Peter Wilberg, *One to One* (Language Teaching Publications)

See also these journals and magazines:

ELT Journal (Oxford University Press)
Practical English Teacher (Mary Glasgow Publications)
Modern English Teacher (Cambridge University Press)

Index

TEACHING ENGLISH GUIDES

Teaching English in Japan *by Jerry O'Sullivan*

Teaching English in Japan was first published in 1992 and has established itself as the leading title in the field. It is an information-packed handbook for teaching and living in Japan and contains substantial information on how to get a job, accommodation, travel and visas, as well as numerous descriptions, tips and suggestions (including model lesson plans and hints on how to deal with specific language problems). 'A manual of practical advice . . . should prove invaluable' *Japan Times*.

Teaching English in Eastern and Central Europe
by Robert Lynes

Teaching English in the countries of the former Eastern Bloc has experienced enormous growth over the last few years. This complete practical guide concentrates on Hungary, the Czech Republic, and Poland. It also covers the Slovak Republic, Romania and Bulgaria. Practical details on how to get work are accompanied by information on the cost of living, accommodation, qualifications, etc. The language problems specific to each country are analysed, making this an ideal classroom manual as well as living guide.

Teaching English in Asia *by Jerry and Nuala O'Sullivan*
Publication: 1996.

From the People's Republic of China to the Indonesian archipelago, the thirst for learning English shows no sign of diminishing. This book covers PR China, Hong Kong, the Indian subcontinent, Indonesia, Japan, South Korea, Malaysia, the Philippines, Singapore, Taiwan, Thailand, and Vietnam. Practical examples of how to get work in each country are given, together with day-to-day living information. The challenges posed in the classrooms of each country are explored, making this a valuable teaching guide as well as an indispensable manual on jobs, prices, etc.

Published in the UK by In Print Publishing Ltd, 9 Beaufort Terrace, Brighton BN2 2SU, UK. Tel: (01273) 682836. Fax: (01273) 620958.

Published in the USA by Passport Books, NTC Publishing Group, 4255 West Touhy Avenue, Lincolnwood (Chicago), IL 60646–1975, USA. Tel: 708 679 5500. Fax: 708 679 6375.